John Collier

Twayne's English Authors Series

Kinley E. Roby, Editor

Northeastern University

TEAS 367

JOHN COLLIER
(1901–1980)
Photograph by John G. S. Collier

John Collier

By Betty Richardson

Southern Illinois University, Edwardsville

Twayne Publishers • *Boston*

John Collier

Betty Richardson

Copyright © 1983 by G.K. Hall & Company
All Rights Reserved
Published by Twayne Publishers
A Division of G. K. Hall & Company
70 Lincoln Street
Boston, Massachusetts 02111

Book Production by Marne B. Sultz

Book Design by Barbara Anderson

Printed on permanent/durable acid-free
paper and bound in the United States of
America.

**Library of Congress Cataloging in
Publication Data**

Richardson, Betty
John Collier.

(Twayne's English authors series; TEAS 367)
Bibliography: p. 116
Includes index.
1. Collier, John, 1901–1980—
Criticism and interpretation.
I. Title. II. Series.
PR6005.036Z85   1983   828'.91209   83-2483
ISBN 0-8057-6853-X

To Louise and Henry Dohle II, to Henry Dohle III, and to Henry and Florence Ax, Terry Cook, Grace and Jack Fish, Marty Komorny and Bob Ketterlin, Irene and Paul Jones, Marlin and Gene Jordan, Troy Matlock, Nancy and Dan Schmidt, Margaret and Roman Stolcis, as well as to those others at Pete Hiney's who have reached out to a stranger with laughter and warmth, wit and affection.

Contents

About the Author

Betty Richardson received the B.A. from the University of Louisville and the M.A. and Ph.D. from the University of Nebraska at Lincoln. She is a professor of English in the Department of English Language and Literature at Southern Illinois University, Edwardsville, where she has also served as departmental chairman. Her previous book, *Sexism in Higher Education,* was published in 1974; and she has published articles, review essays, and reviews in a number of journals, including *Papers on Language and Literature,* the *Bulletin of the Midwest Modern Language Association,* the *AAUP Bulletin, Prairie Schooner,* and *Victorian Studies.*

Preface

John Collier's writing has been widely read for the past fifty years, but his name is not well known among students, teachers, or critics of literature. There are several reasons for this neglect.

First, Collier worked in an unusual variety of literary forms. He began his career as a poet. He next became a novelist, but his work in that genre ended in 1934. During that same period, together with much other occasional writing, he began work on his short stories, and he also collaborated with Iain Lang on a social history of England during the 1920s. In 1935, he left England for Hollywood, and, after that, he was a filmscript and short-story writer. In no single genre did he produce any considerable body of work, and many people who read Collier's stories in such magazines as the *New Yorker* and *Playboy* simply do not associate that apparently contemporary author with the novelist who wrote *His Monkey Wife* some five decades ago.

Second, there is the matter of changing critical tastes. A popular audience of even minimal taste may be lastingly amused by what is amusing, but not so those reviewers who write for newspapers and magazines. Collier's style is light. His wit is diabolical. Neither that style nor that wit was relished amidst the high moral earnestness of the Depression and of World War II. Like Somerset Maugham, Noel Coward, and Virginia Woolf, Collier seemed a dilettantish figure from an earlier age when a light-minded generation of elegant ladies and gentlemen had leisure to indulge itself with subtleties and ironies and style. At the same time, Collier is a clever and iconoclastic social satirist, and, as a human being, he was profoundly cosmopolitan. His writing was compatible with none of the prevailing ideologies of the 1930s and 1940s, and, certainly, he could not be fully appreciated during the politically and socially timid 1950s. By the end of that decade, most of his writing was done.

Third, Collier's general popularity was not calculated to make him popular among academics. His stories have appeared in such anthologies as *Dealer's Choice: The World's Greatest Poker Stories, Murder for the Millions: A*

Harvest of Horror and Homicide, Alfred Hitchcock Presents Stories for Late at Night, and *The Playboy Book of Horror and the Supernatural.* Thus, what Anthony Burgess has called the "puritanism of the scholarly tradition" has been his enemy from the start.[1] Until quite recently, popular literature has been anathematical among academics. During the reign of the New Critics, who demanded that literature be untainted by the things of this world, satirists such as Samuel Butler, Jonathan Swift, and Bernard Shaw could find no place, or only a precarious place, in the academic curriculum, however important or influential they might have been in the world outside. Moreover, these critics and scholars favored literature that is so complex as to be inaccessible to the general public. Their academic opponents were traditionalists—generally, textual and historical scholars. These did not generally favor the introduction of any modern literature at all. Consequently, such writers as Collier simply did not enter into the experience of students of literature.

Fourth, during his long lifetime Collier was a very private person and a very modest one. He was courteous, but he was extraordinarily elusive. Deliberately, he avoided the kind of personal publicity that results in a following; he was genuinely startled when he nonetheless had followers, despite his best efforts to explain to them the folly of their ways. He certainly could not understand why anyone would want to write a book about him.

It is time for John Collier to come into his own. A growing body of scholars and critics respects good writing, whatever its century, politics, or degree of complexity, and there is unprecedented interest today in so-called "popular" literature. John Collier wrote very well indeed, and he is popular. His themes—magic, power, sex, avarice—may have appeared trivial during the Depression and the Holocaust, but they do not seem trivial today; we have had time to recover from those greater catastrophes and turn to contemplate normal, everyday human disasters and brutalities to which Collier's writing has always been quite relevant.

No study of Collier's work presently exists. In order to provide a start, I attempt in this book to synthesize the ideas that consistently inform his work. In Chapter 1, I establish the traditions in which Collier worked and his relationship to his milieu. In Chapter 2, I discuss Collier's last publication, his screenplay of *Paradise Lost.* Collier regarded this work as his most significant. Certainly, while it is a splendid work in its own right, it also summarizes much that he tried to communicate throughout his long writing career. The following chapters offer analysis of Collier's novels with special attention to *His Monkey Wife,* which will probably prove to be his most enduring work. In Chapters 6 and 7, I analyze a selection of his most famous short stories, first studying the forms he commonly used and then his major themes in such a way, I hope, as to provide tools for the study of his many other stories; clearly, it is not possible to discuss all at any length here. Finally, I discuss Collier's vision of his world as seen through his writings.

This will leave much undone, but I will have done what I can do. That I have written this book at all I owe in large part to Carol Keene, formerly Dean of the School of Humanities at Southern Illinois University, Edwardsville. As dean, Dr. Keene gave me released time from some of my teaching duties so that I might begin this book while serving as chairman of a large and extraordinarily active English department. As a friend, she has been consistently and strongly supportive of this effort. I owe thanks, too, to the Graduate School of Southern Illinois University for providing me with a Summer Research Fellowship that allowed me to complete this work. To Marvin Solomon of the university's Lovejoy Library and to several members of the University of Toronto library staff I owe thanks for assistance with my initial research. I wish to thank Paul Jarrico, colleague and friend of John Collier, for the special help and information he gave me, and Howard B. Hunt, Sr., of Louisville, who, by his honorable and laborious handling of personal matters, freed me to complete this manuscript. I own a special debt to my mother, Dora Freiburg Ritchie, and to Dr. Sheila Ruth for their vigorous and generous support, to Martha Komorny for her meticulous editorial help and witty comments during the final preparation of this manuscript, and to Amity Ruth for her editorial assistance.

Finally, I must acknowledge my tremendous debt to the late John Collier and to his family: his son, John G. S. Collier, who contributed the photograph for this book; his sister, Kathleen Mary Collier, who volunteered information about his family, and, above all, his wife, Harriet Hess Collier, whose generosity, graciousness, hospitality, and helpfulness there are no words to describe. I wish it were possible to thank John Collier himself for his willingness, at last, to break his long silence and to speak with me at great length and with great warmth during the months before his death. In his modesty, he rejected out of hand as outrageous the notion that any reputable company would choose to publish a book about him; I only wish he could have lived to see the publication of this one. Despite his physical weakness, he was generous, charming, witty, and wise during the hours I spent with him. It was both a privilege and a pleasure to have been granted that time; those hours from beginning to end were a joy and a delight.

Betty Richardson

Southern Illinois University, Edwardsville

Acknowledgments

Quotations from *Defy the Foul Fiend,* copyright 1934 by John Collier, © renewed 1961 by John Collier, are reprinted by permission of the Harold Matson Company, Inc.

Quotations from *Fancies and Goodnights,* copyright 1951 by John Collier, © renewed 1979 by John Collier, are reprinted by permission of the Harold Matson company, Inc.

Quotations from *His Monkey Wife,* copyright 1931 by John Collier, © renewed 1958, are reprinted by permission of the Harold Matson Company, Inc.

Quotations from *The John Collier Reader,* © 1972 by Alfred A. Knopf, Inc., are reprinted by permission of the publisher and of the Harold Matson Company, Inc.

Quotations from *Paradise Lost,* © 1973 by John Collier, are reprinted by permission of the Harold Matson Company, Inc.

Quotations from *The Scandal and Credulities of John Aubrey,* copyright 1931 by John Collier, © renewed 1959 by John Collier, are reprinted by permission of the Harold Matson Company, Inc.

Quotation from John Collier's preface to *The Gourmet's Almanac* is by permission of Thomas Harmsworth Publishing.

Quotation from Christopher Isherwood's unpublished comments on *Paradise Lost* is printed by permission of the author.

Quotations from Paul Jarrico's unpublished "Some Thoughts About John Collier" are printed by permission of the author.

Quotations from Tom Milne, "The Elusive John Collier," *Sight and Sound* 45 (Spring 1976) are reprinted by permission of *Sight and Sound.*

Quotations from reviews of *His Monkey Wife, Times Literary Supplement,* 5 February 1931, and of *Tom's A-Cold, Times Literary Supplement,* 27 April 1933, are reprinted by permission of the *London Times Literary Supplement.*

Quotation from "Hoot Owl at Large" is by permission of *Time,* the Weekly Newsmagazine, copyright Time Inc., 1941.

Quotation from C. J. Eustace review of *Defy the Foul Fiend* is used by permission of *Canadian Forum.*

JOHN COLLIER

Chronology

land," "Another American Tragedy," and "Over Insurance."

1940   *Witch's Money;* stories including "Old Acquaintance," "If Youth Knew, If Age Could," "The Steel Cat," "Meeting of Relations," "Bird of Prey," "The Touch of Nutmeg Makes It," and "Spring Fever."

1941   Traveled throughout United States; wrote "Three Bears Cottage," "Interpretation of a Dream," "Incident on a Lake," and "De Mortuis"; *Presenting Moonshine* (short-story collection).

1942   Moved to California; *Her Cardboard Lover* (film).

1943   *The Touch of Nutmeg and More Unlikely Stories.*

1946   *Deception* (film).

1949   *Roseanna McCoy* (film).

1951   *Fancies and Goodnights* (short-story collection).

1953   Wrote "Equilibrium," "Jealous Lover," and "Mademoiselle" episodes for *The Story of Three Loves;* left United States for Mexico, later settling in France.

1954   Married Harriet Hess in Mexico, 25 May.

1955   *I Am a Camera* (film); "A Matter of Taste" and "The Tender Age"; purchased Domaine du Blanchissage in Grasse, France, which remained his home until 1979.

1958   Son, John G. S. Collier, born in Nice; *Pictures in the Fire;* "Asking for It" and "Softly Walks the Beetle."

1965   *The War Lord* (film).

1971   Production of *His Monkey Wife* as musical in London with music by Sandy Wilson.

1972   *The John Collier Reader.*

1973   *Milton's Paradise Lost.*

1975   *The Best of John Collier* (abridged reissue of *The John Collier Reader*).

1979   Returned from France to live in Santa Monica and later Pacific Palisades.

1980   Died 6 April.

Chapter One
Life, Literature, and Milieu

On 22 January 1901, Queen Victoria died at Osborne. In the United States, a woman's suffrage group was founded at Radcliffe College, but this was still an era of feminine elegance, especially in the England of Edward VII. In America and across the English channel, there were, however, other portents of changes to come. A new kind of music—ragtime—was making itself known in America, and Theodore Roosevelt was introducing a new kind of presidential style. On the Continent, Picasso was entering his Blue Period. But these developments seemed remote from England at the beginning of the brief Edwardian age, an age which was to mark the end of traditional Victorian verities and decorums.

On 3 May 1901, John Collier was born into an England still more or less at peace, for, although the Boer War may well have been England's Vietnam, it in no way can be compared with the conflicts that would begin in 1914. In "Excuse in Autumn," a poem in *Gemini,* his 1931 volume of verse, Collier looked back wistfully at the serenity of the prewar landscape:

> To be a whole Nineteen-eleven family
> Living at Golders Green with a red wall,
> Spring joy crocus, young child-drawn almond tree,
> In Autumn sea of mauve daisies filling all[1]

Collier was never to lose his nostalgia for the old pastoral landscapes of England. Speaking in 1979, he could still imagine no better life than that of an English country gentleman.[2]

The family into which Collier was born was an established one. A great-grandfather had been physician to William IV and George IV; various of his descendants were known for their work in the arts and in medicine.[3] During Collier's childhood, an uncle, Vincent Collier, attempted to establish himself as a writer of fiction. Now long forgotten, he was to publish at least one novel; *Light Fingers and Dark Eyes* appeared in London during 1913.

Unfortunately, John Collier's father, born in 1852, was one of seventeen children. He was the oldest, and, because of a complicated domestic situation, he became responsible for the rest. As was then often the case with such enormous families, there was not money enough to make each child secure. Consequently, Collier's father was so poor as to be forced to find employment as a clerk in an office, then considered a demeaning position for a gentleman.

Young Collier's education was, as a result, highly irregular. He recalled a kindergarten where, at three, he began reading the fairy tales of Hans Christian Andersen. He early found reading to be an "absolutely fascinating" activity, and the fairy tales left so lasting an impression that, decades later, he was to return to their motifs when writing stories of his own. He also read penny books for children, mostly, he recollected, about "titans." So convincing were these stories and so vivid was the child's imagination that he remembered huddling atop a kitchen table for fear that some ogre might be lurking beneath it. His mother introduced him to Charles Kingsley's *Water Babies* while he was still quite young, and this 1863 children's fantasy dealing with morality and evolution became "the first real writing I had read."

Victorian Values

Insofar as Collier was systematically educated, he was principally educated by his novelist uncle, Vincent Collier, although John Collier recalled studying with a tutor. He also recalled that a butcher's boy was called into the kitchen to instruct him into the mysteries of long division and that he was "much educated" by an eight-year-old friend who introduced him to *A Midsummer Night's Dream.* Primarily, he was given a literary education, and that education typified the values and tastes of a middle-class world still dominated by the great Victorians.

In the world of Collier's childhood, those writers whom we now regard as Victorian were still responsible for most major literary events. In the year of Collier's birth, Rudyard Kipling published *Kim* and Conan Doyle's "Hound of the Baskervilles" was serialized in the *Strand.* In 1902, Kipling's *Just So Stories* appeared. Meredith and Swinburne were nearing the end of their lives, but Chesterton and Belloc were at the height of their powers. Bernard Shaw was the most prolific of England's social critics, as well as the foremost figure of the stage; as critic, H. G. Wells would have ranked second. Samuel Butler's modestly rebellious *The Way of All Flesh*

appeared posthumously two years after Collier's birth and seemed startlingly fresh and daring to a generation of young men who would claim to
be influenced by it. In 1906, John Galsworthy published *The Man of
Property,* the first of the Forsyte tales, and, in 1908, Arnold Bennett
produced *The Old Wives' Tale.* England remained splendidly isolated from
the intellectual ferment of the Continent. Although Constance Garnett
had completed her translation of Turgenev as early as 1899, even the
importance of the great Russian writers was not to be recognized for
almost another decade, and such self-proclaimed cosmopolitans as Henry James actually offered no rude shocks to conventional English
sensibilities.

Naturally, then, Collier's education was insular. At one point, a tutor
encouraged him to read Wordsworth. Collier admired "Intimations of
Immortality," and from there he went on to read Tennyson, whom he also
respected. Under Vincent Collier's tutelage, he read and enjoyed Homer
and Dryden's edition of Virgil as well as works by Pope and Gray. The boy
found the eighteenth century to be compatible with his own temperament, and he later read widely in the works of Defoe, Steele, Fielding,
Sterne, and Smollett. He was required to imitate Pope's style, and,
afterwards, he continued to fall easily into the cadences of eighteenth-
century rhetoric. His novel *Defy the Foul Fiend* derives from that age in
both substance and tone.

Most important, Collier claimed, were the books he read for pleasure.
On his own, he read the novels of Thackeray and Dickens, the picaresque
stories of Robert Smith Surtees, and the adventure stories of Frederick
Marryat. Rabelais, he said, was profoundly important to him as was
Charles Kingsley's last novel, *Hereward the Wake,* based on a legendary
account of an outlaw who led a rebellion against William the Conqueror.
In his teens, he discovered Charles Darwin's *Origin of Species,* James Frazer's
Golden Bough, the final volume of which appeared in 1915, and Edward
Gibbon's *Decline and Fall of the Roman Empire,* the latter a lasting source of
reading pleasure. His discovery of John Stuart Mill turned his thoughts
toward socialism.

During the twilight before World War I, then, it was possible for a boy
to learn those moral certainties that make possible the writing of social
satire. Trusting the eighteenth century's right reason, he discerned a point
of view from which he would mock those who take fashionable society too
seriously in *His Monkey Wife* and those who take the self too seriously in
Defy the Foul Fiend. When Collier turns his attention to the shoddiness,

avarice, and mechanized lust of the twentieth century, his wit bites with the force of the great satirists and Victorian seers upon whose writing he was raised.

A Period of Change

Somewhere between December 1910 and Armistice Day 1919, "human character changed," or so Virginia Woolf claimed when she fixed the date of change firmly in 1910.[4] In that, she may have exaggerated, but, certainly, the period marked dramatic political, social, and cultural shifts in England, as elsewhere. It was not only Edward VII who died in 1910; an entire generation of those who shared attitudes commonly regarded as Victorian died away, including, in that same year, Mark Twain, Leo Tolstoy, and Florence Nightingale. In England, many changes were marked by violence. In 1909, more than 100 women were arrested when these suffragettes lay siege to the House of Commons, throwing rocks and battling policemen. Later, Irish patriots rebelled, and working men grew mutinous. War broke out, and domestic servants left their employment for higher-paying jobs in factories from which they never returned. The social order would never be the same.

Neither would the arts. A young generation demanded that artists climb down from their pedestals and depict reality in the language of truth. This demand, of course, had been familiar since the time of Wordsworth, but, during the teens of this century, it was restated because truth and reality were themselves taking on new and exciting forms. What Virginia Woolf originally had in mind when dating the change from 1910 was the Post-Impressionist exhibition arranged by Roger Fry, which introduced London to the painting of Van Gogh, Cézanne, and Matisse. There were many other manifestations of a changing reality. In 1911, the Russian Ballet opened in London, while, on Christmas Eve of 1912, a review called *Hullo Rag-Time!* opened at the London Hippodrome and ran for 451 performances, delighting such young writers as Rupert Brooke. In Russia, a film was made of *Anna Karenina,* and, by 1912, films had ceased to be mere novelties; there were 400 cinemas in London alone. British culture, which had previously been conspicuous for its resistance to foreign influence, could not withstand such onslaughts, even before it underwent the trauma produced by the carnage of World War I.

Collier came to maturity during the war years. He determined to become a poet, although, he recalled, his father turned pale when he made known his desire. Despite his reservations, the older Collier dutifully installed his son in Pimlico with an income of £100 a year, enough to subsidize a romantically bohemian existence, and the father continued to help the son for many years. John Collier remained in London as a poet, journalist, and writer from the middle 1920s through the end of that decade. He clearly was exhilarated by his participation in the ferment of his time.

Just the Other Day

Collier relived his excitement when he collaborated with Iain Lang to write *Just the Other Day: An Informal History of Great Britain Since the War,* published in 1932. Collier and Lang claimed to be modeling their effort on Frederick Lewis Allen's *Only Yesterday: An Informal History of the Nineteen-Twenties,*[5] but the Collier and Lang volume differs in the quality of exuberance that shines through the magisterial tone they chose to adopt. Collier's contributions, as he remembered them, were primarily the chapters dealing with literature and the arts, but his peculiar wit shows in other sections of the book so that only in a few sections is it clearly possible to distinguish between the contributions of the two authors.

Collier and Lang look back to the literary world prior to 1919 as a "peaceful landscape" in which even Georgian poets—poets such as W. H. Davies, Rupert Brooke, and Lascelles Abercrombie, who were uncontroversial in content and simple in style—could be "popularly accepted as progressive youth."[6] By 1919, they note, this landscape "was in the first throes of an earthquake" (224). The nature of this upheaval was such as to cause literature to "evolve from the imitative to the interpretive stage" (244). Collier and Lang are sympathetic toward the leaders in this evolutionary process. Of James Joyce and *Ulysses,* which they describe as a work of genius, they write: "As early as 1919 a woman, Dorothy Richardson, had seen the possibilities for literary art of a reproduction in words of given 'streams of consciousness.' But Joyce added a musical technique of changes of key, recapitulation and orchestral effects of all descriptions to this idea." The authors are impatient with critics who stress the "recondite origins of Joyce's patterns and eccentricities," saying that these critics "obscured the very qualities" that would otherwise attract a more general audience. Actually, Joyce's great achievement involves his "magnificent powers of creating character, his astonishing stock of information on everyday affairs, his innumerable and vivid pictures of the familiar sordidness of streets, and his rapid Rabelaisian humour. . . ." More important than his technical achievements, these qualities will be "prized long after his experiments have failed, and become out-of-date oddities, or succeeded, and become matters of course" (231).

They also single out Edith, Osbert, and Sacheverell Sitwell. In 1979, Collier recalled first reading the 1919 and 1920 issues of Edith Sitwell's annual anthology *Wheels;* "that was a new world for me," he said. Collier apparently was impressed by the poetic synthesis of modernism with the historical and literary traditions to which the Sitwells, with their 600 years of family history, fell heir, although this is not apparent in the Collier and Lang volume. In *Just the Other Day,* the authors merely observe that the Sitwells' interest in Continental music and painting, in individualism, and in "new and abstract values" might well have been pose "had it not so frequently flashed with genius" (227). They cite Edith Sitwell's "Sleeping Beauty" and Sacheverell Sitwell's "Hundred and One Harlequins," among others, for their purity and exquisiteness. And they prefer, they say, the gaiety of the Sitwells to the "ecclesiastical accent" of T. S. Eliot and the "cathedral atmosphere" of the school of poetry that he founded (228). Still, the voice of a conservative tradition is heard when Collier and Lang sum up the achievements of these new writers, finding their work, in the long run, not so divorced as its practitioners might believe from that of John Donne, Robert Browning, the picaresque novelists, and George Meredith (236).

While their tastes are eclectic, they are contemptuous of that which seems fashionable and shoddy. They regard the genius of Chaplin and Eisenstein as indisputable, and they are impressed by the "cinemato-graphic effects" of John Dos Passos (236). They praise Lytton Strachey for his debunking of history, writing that his *Queen Victoria* must delight "all but the most unimaginatively reverent" (233). However, with an austerity worthy of an earlier generation, they sternly pass judgment on stage productions by Noel Coward and by Somerset Maugham, seeing these writers as pandering to the prurient self-indulgence and vulgarity as-sociated with the decade's Bright Young Things and Flappers. Of Coward's *Vortex,* with its unchaste mother and drug-addicted son, they observe: "If youth was no better than it should be—and it had no intention of being better—the responsibility, in moments of remorseful hysteria, was passed on to the elder generation: if young people could not, without violence to reason, honour father and mother, why should they put themselves to the inconvenience of obeying the other commandments?" Of Maugham's *Our Betters,* they severely note that it represents "fashionable maturity as a dreary routine of passionless and haphazard lechery" (127). A similar disgust appears in two of Collier's novels, *His Monkey Wife* and *Defy the Foul Fiend,* and in many of the short stories.

To some extent, Collier, in writing such criticism, allies himself with what Martin Green has described as the *Sonnenkinder* ("Children of the Sun"), who, as rogues, as aesthetes, as *naifs,* or as dandies rejected the principles of their father's generation, a generation whose veneration for traditional concepts had brought down the First World War upon the heads of their sons.[7] Often avant-garde and witty, they were heirs to nineteenth-century notions of dandyism and aestheticism and were deeply influenced by the traditional figures—Columbine, Pierrot, Harlequin— of the Italian *commedia dell'arte* and by the Dionysian energies of Sergei Diaghilev's Russian Ballet productions. According to Green, they included such dandies and dandy-aesthetes as the three Sitwells, Virginia Woolf, and Cecil Beaton, and such political *naifs* as Christopher Isherwood. Certainly, Collier shared certain attitudes and influences; he was stirred by Diaghilev's ballet and, for example, adopted the Harlequin figure as the rakish devil of a number of his short stories. But Collier apparently never fully identified with any of the London literary sets or figures that he moved among after the success of *His Monkey Wife.* He could not, for there was in him a conflict between the avant-garde intellectual and the traditional English squire. He spelled out the nature of the conflict in his first and only book of poems.

Gemini

The twins of the title are Orson and Valentine, twin elements of the poet's personality as well as the twins of the zodiac, the man of action and the man of thought. That both voices are real, Collier writes, "I know . . . from having lived in them very wholly and intensely for some years. . . ."[8] Orson is the voice of "something archaic, uncouth, and even barbarous," while Valentine's is the voice of "an hysterically self-conscious dandy" (1). In all probability, the names are borrowed from an early French romance that appeared in England about 1550 as the *History of Two Valyannte Brethren, Valentyne and Orson.* In the original tale, Orson is carried away by a bear and raised as a wild man; he is eventually discovered and tamed by his brother Valentine, who has been raised as a knight. In Collier's depiction of the conflict between the two facets of personality represented by these voices, neither is ever quite tamed.

Gemini contains eight pieces of writing. It begins with a seven-page prose "Apology" and an introductory poem, "Address to the Worms." This is followed by "Three Men in One Room," which is intended to represent the voice of Orson. This eleven-page poem is followed by four short poems told in the voice of Valentine: "Oh Soul Be Chang'd into Little Water Drops," "Sunday Morning," "Excuse in Autumn," and "Brookside Reverie (Or Mind over Matter)." The volume ends with a four-page prose passage entitled "Of Consolation through Murder."

Like *Just the Other Day,* this volume reveals an intense reaction to the influences of the 1920s. As a poet, Collier later described himself as "imitative as a monkey," but little of the verse indeed seems to be purely imitative. Rather, Collier possessed a collector's instinct, gathering for himself the finest bits of style and most glittering images from what he found around him. His poetry is an excited reaction to the literary commotion of his time by a young man gifted with great sensitivity to language, a rare facility for mimicry, and a high measure of stylistic virtuosity of his own.

In his "Apology," Collier praises Edith Sitwell, this time saying that she alone of modern poets is "completely successful in verse" because her "intellectual processes and her aesthetic emotions are nearly related, and can use the same word . . . " (7). Collier seems here to be trying for similar effects with the result that his meaning is sometimes similarly elusive. Still, there are signs that he was influenced by many other writers. More than a touch of Donne is to be found in "Address to the Worms," in which the poet describes himself as "The man in worm, your deity" (9). In the words quoted earlier from "Excuse in Autumn"—"Spring joy crocus, young child-drawn almond tree"—Collier seems to be showing the influence of Gerard Manley Hopkins. Poets from Pope to Eliot leave traces in "Three Men in One Room," the most interesting and least effective poem in the volume.

"Three Men in One Room" has both great strengths and weaknesses. The strengths are those that will turn a minor writer of verse into a brilliant writer of fantastical prose. In this poem, a world division, distinctly Prufrockian although it is supposed to be that of the "rough cub" Orson, is confined to an occasionally too rigorous couplet form:

> . . . that aged one
> Who, bearded like black frost, clad in old brown,
> Drifts, a bent autumn leaf, reluctant, down
> Pimlico streets towards the Styx, yet will

> Abate no vice of youth, save one, though still
> His ailings cluster, and his gait, words, breath
> Lampoon old age, reproach unpunctual death. (12)

Most effective are those passages in which Collier develops mood and tone in outlandish images:

> Bones, ashes and decay strew all the floor:
> Where the dim light, for skulls, false teeth reveals,
> And restless ghosts, who live on ghosts of meals;
> Where the dark ceiling like a thunder-cloud
> Broods, and each blanket seems a twice-used shroud. (11)

Delight in language, metaphor, and rhyme often takes control of the poetry at the expense of substance and coherence, an error that Collier will rarely make in his later writing.

The Valentine poems provide sharp contrast to "Three Men in One Room." In these, we catch the tone of Swinburne and Dowson as when, in "Oh Soul Be Chang'd into Little Water Drops," Collier writes:

> He has given himself over to a lack of names
> Who when he was all words must make each strong
> He names neither grief nor heart nor joy nor weeping
> Pain nor wrong. (23)

Of these poems, "Excuse in Autumn" is most successful.

Gemini, however, is the culmination, not the beginning, of Collier's career as a poet. As early as 1922, Collier had won a poetry prize from *This Quarter,* and, in the "Apology" to *Gemini,* he indicates that he is turning away from poetry because in verse he cannot synthesize the voices of Orson and Valentine. He says that he has taken his first lesson in prose from *Ulysses,* "that city of modern prose," and that, having done so, he has found a "language in which Valentine and Orson can become one . . . " (6–7).

Ultimately, Joyce's syntax was certainly not to become Collier's own vehicle, but the immediate result of Collier's admiration was the clever, extremely imitative "Of Consolation through Murder," which concludes *Gemini.* In it, Collier reveals a close study of Joyce's mode of creating character and his knowledge of the everyday happenings of mean streets, both Joycean qualities praised in *Just the Other Day:*

> Annie, two mousey years his wife, stalled off with
> please oh please his ginger smell, his china coney
> eye, drawn joints and ribs furrowed on a high jut
> white as death. My wife, he said, words falling on
> the tepid sick-breath of his drugshop, my wife is
> highly strung. Yet in his brain a covert lecher
> stirred beneath cost price sale price and orris
> smell of peaky high-flown love. (30)

The title of this piece, however, suggests that DeQuincey and Wilde vied with Joyce for Collier's attention, and also brings to mind some themes of the fiction to come, much of which was to deal with domestic mayhem in a variety of forms.

The Novels

At the end of the 1920s, Collier tired of the "squalors of the city" and retired to the country. He was already writing regularly in a variety of forms. By the time *Gemini* appeared, Collier had published his first and most important novel, *His Monkey Wife,* which created a stir in literary London. But, as Collier recalled the event, publication of the first novel was a by-product of other writing projects.

He imposed his wit and style upon a variety of unlikely subjects. Among his writings, for example, is a preface to a whimsically titled volume on English cooking compiled by Allan Ross Macdougall: *The Gourmet's Almanac: Wherein is set down . . . recipes for strange and exotic dishes with divers considerations anent the cooking and the eating thereof, together with . . . the words and music of such old-fashioned songs as should be sung by all proud and lusty fellows.* The traditionalism of the man in love with the land makes its presence felt in Collier's preface. He writes: "We can turn time on the spit, baste with the past, season with the centuries. Who roasts a pike, having stuffed it with anchovies and oysters, dines with Walton, and that's only the narrowest way of it. For he who chooses his surloin with understanding, and goes to greet it in the kitchen, doing it honour in the eyes of his cook, that man eats with England."[9]

He also edited an edition of John Aubrey's seventeenth-century *Brief Lives* under a new title, *The Scandal and Credulities of John Aubrey.* Here, too, Collier emphasizes the richness and fullness of old English life, claiming that the edition then standard, the work of Andrew Clark, had sacrificed this rich texture, with its aesthetic truth, to the dryness of scholarship. It is typical of Collier, also, to insist upon a virtually unexpurgated edition, saying, "I have omitted no unseemly passage which I consider either important or beautiful or amusing, and such was the seventeenth century in the first case, and such is life in the second, and such am I in the third case, that I have chosen to leave out only one paragraph, and I am not sure that I am right in doing that."[10]

In preparation for the Aubrey edition, Collier read at the Bodleian Library and consulted with his publisher, to whom he remarked that he had written a novel. The publisher read *His Monkey Wife* and brought it out.

In his country retreat, Collier then devoted himself to nature, hunting, and fiction. Only occasionally did he visit London thereafter, despite the opportunities offered after publication of *His Monkey Wife,* and he lost touch with a life that once had attracted him. "My world was a world of country life," he reminisced. "I very rarely went to town." When he did, he recalled, he took tea once or twice with Edith Sitwell, and he remembered occasionally dining with Osbert Sitwell and infrequent meetings with E. M. Forster, Wyndham Lewis, Dora Carrington, friend of Lytton Strachey, and her husband, Ralph Partridge. But much of his earlier excitement had faded. In a sense, Orson had for a time conquered Valentine.

His Monkey Wife. Publication of *His Monkey Wife* amply proved that Collier was "a writer speaking, a writer's writer, a serious writer," as his friend Paul Jarrico described him in "Some Thoughts About John Collier."[11] *His Monkey Wife* was and remains influential among other writers; Julian Moynahan, in a 1979 review of a volume of Ian McEwan stories, is among the more recent to report an author who probably owes a debt to John Collier's "charming literary jape."[12] At the time of publication, some reviewers were enthusiastic, heralding the novel as an extraordinary first effort and praising its "subtle wit," "beauty," and "penetrating satire."[13]

Despite these reviews and despite the stir created in literary London, for all practical purposes the book appeared at the wrong time. To be generally perceived as both a fantasist and an important novelist, Collier was born too late. Others who achieved great popular and critical recognition for their fantasies were older writers; G. K. Chesterton was born in 1874, Max Beerbohm in 1872, and Virginia Woolf in 1882. Maturing before World War I, they produced their fantasies before Black Friday and the rise of fascism caused the mood of the reading public in general to become more sober.

Witty and gay, *His Monkey Wife* was published just when the effects of the stock-market crash were beginning to be felt around the world, when the mood of the intellectuals suddenly darkened. As Stephen Spender observes, the 1930s were a period of mounting crisis and at such a time "every work takes on a political look in either being symptomatic of that crisis . . . or in avoiding it."[14] Light fantasy had no place in such a world; light cynicism about fashionable society gave the appearance of gross insensitivity, and sex and sexual roles were put aside, not to be considered of political importance for another thirty years. Very quickly, comic writers—even, in the eyes of some, Bernard Shaw and Charles Dickens—were perceived to be shallow and second rate. Satire must be laced with bitterness; Sinclair Lewis's *Babbitt* (1922) won the 1930 Nobel Prize.

Critics reacted accordingly. The *New Republic* reviewer found "less humor than artifice,"[15] while a writer for the *Saturday Review* complained that the satire lacked Swift's "fierce indignation against human vileness. . . ."[16] The *Times Literary Supplement* reported that "Mr. Collier is obviously entirely indifferent to the feelings of his readers, and it is not only the squeamish who will object to certain passages. . . ."[17] Searching for a political message, this critic interpreted the satires as a "bitter and effective antifeminist" attack. It is not.

Tom's A-Cold.   Collier better adapted his handling of fantasy to the mood of the times in his second novel, *Tom's A-Cold,* published in 1933; it appeared in the United States under the title *Full Circle*. In 1979, Collier described this book as "silly" and "very naive," regretting that too many of its possibilities went unrealized. He said that when he began to perceive the threat of another major war he decided to write an essay to show what would happen if conflicts continued. The essay became a novel. In portraying England as it might be in 1995, Collier envisioned a land so devastated by a series of wars that it is reduced to a primitive, brutal tribal society.

Collier had caught the earnest tone of his age, and the book was generally well received. While a *New Statesman* critic regretted that Collier had sacrificed his comic talent to what another reviewer termed an interest that "is entirely and of necessity sociological,"[18] *Tom's A-Cold* moved Osbert Sitwell to compare it with William Faulkner's *Light in August*. Collier and Faulkner, according to Sitwell, "hold more promise than any of their fellow-writers of to-day." Both novels are sensational, but their sensationalism is of the kind that, "exploding like a bomb, opens the mind, blasting holes and passages and tunnels through conventional thought."[19] Still another reviewer hailed the novel as a brilliant piece of work by a serious philosophical mind, noting that it "is not only one of the best but also the best written novel I have come across this year."[20] Iris Barry, reviewing the novel for *Books,* called it a "first-rate narrative" with "rich unforgettable characters in it whose desires and actions alike convince and surprise one."[21] The reviewer for the *Times Literary Supplement* this time was pleased: "The fantastic is never far from Mr. Collier's pen; but here, while it is given just sufficient scope to bring out the best in him, the theme he has chosen prevents it from jogging his elbow too violently."[22]

    Defy the Foul Fiend.   Collier's final novel was the picaresque *Defy the Foul Fiend,* published in 1934. He wrote the novel, he said, in three weeks, with a day and a half out for pheasant shooting, then "my principal preoccupation." He stayed in bed, writing in pencil, and a willing woman friend conveyed the manuscript pages in batches to a pheasant-shooting companion who knew how to type. *Defy the Foul Fiend,* Collier remarked, indeed reflected his preoccupations with the joys and usages of rural English life, "principally murder."

    Although the charge of frivolity recurred, reviewers generally agreed that Collier had once again harnessed his imagination and put it to the service of a serious kind of literature. Writing for *Canadian Forum,* C. J. Eustace commented: "His style is so artificial, and his situations so removed from life, that at times one is tempted to dismiss him lightly. But he makes us think. He is unpleasantly direct. In his way he *is* a genius. . . ."[23] Wyndham Lewis, reviewing for the *Spectator,* approved Collier's insistence that his hero take the responsibility for the consequences of his actions.[24] Peter Quennell for the *New Statesman* and the critic for the *Times Literary Supplement* alike found the book overly mannered, while the *Saturday Review* writer discovered too much of "quaintness" in it.[25] The *Chicago Daily Tribune* reviewer, on the other hand, fully recognized and appreciated Collier's "dazzling" and "blindingly brilliant" style.[26] Collier had shown similar virtuosity in *His Monkey Wife;* again, the darker tone of this later work was better in keeping with the mood of the time.

The Short Stories

Collier began to write short stories in 1926 while he still lived in London. A friend, E. X. Kapp, had an enormous studio just off the

Haymarket. When Kapp went to Antigua, Collier recalled, he offered Collier use of the studio provided Collier paid a servant's salary. To Collier's horror, that salary was almost equal to Collier's annual income. To survive, he gave parties to which people brought things to eat and drink. What they left, he ate. Someone brought a typewriter to one of these parties, and he pecked out parts of the story "Green Thoughts" on this machine. He wrote another story on the way to visit his friend in Antigua; this story was submitted to the *Dial*. His friend insisted on sending a third tale to the *New Yorker*. Collier was amazed at the response: "Out of nowhere came this writer who wrote these stories, and it was me." Eventually, he found that once he had fully shaped the first sentence, the rest of the story would seem to develop of its own accord.

Most of the important stories were written between 1937 and 1939, and many of these, he insisted, were written quickly for money, since money remained a problem. As Paul Jarrico observes, Collier found it "difficult" to take "serious things seriously": "John had no respect for money. Not that he didn't need it. There were times he needed it desperately. But he had no respect for it." Jarrico continues: "He was profligate on principle, improvident on purpose. In part this was the result of his upbringing. . . . A gentleman is not a merchant—he has a different relation to money. He scorns it because he has it. And if he loses it, the scorn persists. Life is a gamble. Win or lose, a gentleman is blase. Or at least pretends to be."[27] Collier's gift for the short-story form provided him with a certain degree of security; he wrote more stories during another period of exigency in the 1950s.

Publication of the stories in book form began in 1931 with *No Traveler Returns,* followed by *Green Thoughts* (1932), *The Devil and All* (1934), and *Variation on a Theme* (1935). Several of these early publications—e.g., *Variation on a Theme*—were elegant, slim volumes containing a single story, but *The Devil and All* contained some of his most famous tales including "The Possession of Angela Bradshaw," "The Right Side," "Halfway to Hell," "The Devil George and Rosie," and "Hell Hath No Fury." Most of the remainder were collected in *Presenting Moonshine* (1941), *The Touch of Nutmeg and More Unlikely Stories* (1943), and *Pictures in the Fire* (1958). Currently, *Fancies and Goodnights* (1951) and *The Best of John Collier* (1972) serve to keep his most important stories in print.

There are about fifty stories in all, most of them published in such journals and magazines as the *New Yorker, Playboy, Yale Review, Atlantic Monthly, Esquire, Harper's Bazaar, Harper's Magazine, Fantasy and*

Science Fiction, and *Ellery Queen's Mystery Magazine.* "Green Thoughts" was apparently the first story to be anthologized, appearing in Dashiell Hammett's 1931 collection *Creeps By Night,* and fifty years later the stories are still regularly appearing in collections; among the most recent are the inclusion of "Wet Saturday" in Joan Kahn's *Some Things Dark and Dangerous* and of "The Love Connoisseur" in *The Fifties* volume of the Ellery Queen series *Masterpieces of Mystery.*[28] There have been many foreign-language translations, and his stories are regularly reprinted abroad, especially, in recent years, in Japan.

Critical reception of the stories has been mixed, as if in this case the general popularity of Collier's writing must, in some manner, throw his seriousness as a writer into question; only now are his stories beginning to find their way into college literature texts. What most irritated Collier was the persistent association of his stories with those of H. H. Monro ("Saki"), with the implication that he had deliberately chosen Saki as his model. Even in an introduction to a Collier anthology, *The Touch of Nutmeg,* Clifton Fadiman insists that Collier's skill is like that "negligent and foppish genius" of Saki, somewhat unobservantly arguing, also, that Collier is not a "thinker or a close observer of humankind," but rather that he has "the genuine *soufflé* touch."[29] Collier insisted that he read nothing by Saki until 1939 when he briefly visited Ireland. Browsing in a bookstore, Collier examined some Saki stories and decided that he could do something along those lines. The result was "Thus I Refute Beelzy." "So much for my discipleship to Saki," concluded Collier.

There have been other literary associations, not all of them flattering. Reviewing *The Touch of Nutmeg* for the *New York Times,* Marjorie Farber noted that the stories sometimes resemble "overripe O. Henry," although this reviewer is conscious of his "moral ends" and of "the deft conviction of a poet."[30] A reviewer of *Presenting Moonshine* was rather more comprehensive, pointing to Saki, Lord Dunsany, S. J. Perelman, Anatole France, Sax Rohmer, and James Branch Cabell.[31] Other critics were more perceptive. A reviewer for *Time* wrote: "Author John Collier is crazy as a hoot owl. But perched in the gnarled limb of satire, he blinks down with dry wisdom at a world much crazier than he. Effortlessly he glides into madness."[32] Most sensitive is fellow writer Anthony Burgess in his introduction to *The Best of John Collier:* "Read his short stories and you will see all the script-writer's virtues—intense economy, characterization through speech, the sharp camera-eye of observation. You will also find literature, grace, allusiveness, erudition, the artist as well as the craftsman."[33]

Hollywood

In the 1930s, Collier again felt financial pressure. He sold his English property and moved to France. In Cassis, a seaport town near Marseilles, he found a boat that he wanted to buy and remodel. For this, he recalled, he needed 7,000 francs, and he did not have any such sum. At that moment, thanks to introductions arranged for him by Hugh Walpole,[34] he was offered a chance to write a Hollywood script. The $500 salary would permit him to buy the boat. According to Collier in a 1976 interview with Tom Milne, "I was off like a shot."[35]

During the next thirty years, he was to write parts or all of the scripts for *Sylvia Scarlett* (1936), *Elephant Boy* (1937), *Her Cardboard Lover* (1942), *Deception* (1946), *Roseanna McCoy* (1949), *The Story of Three Loves* (1953), *I Am a Camera* (1955), and *The War Lord* (1965). He was also responsible for the original script for *The African Queen;* the final version is occasionally and wrongly attributed to him. He was first to realize the potential of the C. S. Forester novel. He brought it to the attention of Jack Warner, who initially agreed to film the book but later terminated the project. Collier's draft for the film did not include a wedding between the characters eventually played by Humphrey Bogart and Katharine Hepburn.

In the period after the Depression, Hollywood was an economic mecca, attracting the best in literary talent. William Faulkner went there in 1932; F. Scott Fitzgerald had tried film writing as early as 1927, finally moving to Hollywood to work for MGM in 1937. Walpole himself had gone to Hollywood in 1934; his first script was *David Copperfield.* As cinematic methods were polished in the 1920s and 1930s and as these more sophisticated techniques demanded long and coherent scripts, there was a tendency to adapt literary works then deemed significant or classic. Inevitably, many of these works were British: *Lady Windermere's Fan* (1925), *Dr. Jekyll and Mr. Hyde* (1933), *Of Human Bondage* (1934), *Pygmalion* (1938), *David Copperfield* (1935), *Becky Sharp* (1935), and *The Thirty-Nine Steps* (1935), to name only a very few examples. British writers were in demand long before Hitler forced the growth of an international colony at the end of the decade.

Looking back on his career at the time of his 1976 and 1979 interviews, Collier saw much of it as a series of lost opportunities. Originally, he was given a chance to work with George Cukor, who had escorted Walpole to California. Cukor had begun his career on Broadway and had directed such stars as Ethel Barrymore and Laurette Taylor. Collier regarded him as a sensitive and brilliant director; his film credits before Collier's arrival included A *Bill of Divorcement, Dinner at Eight,* and *Little Women.*

Collier blamed himself for what he regarded as an unsatisfactory script for *Sylvia Scarlett,* although, as was customary, he worked with a team of writers. The film and his later career might have been rewarding, he said, "if I'd had the sense to learn all I might have learned from Cukor." Instead, he said, he was "ignorant and arrogant," and he refused to take films seriously or to learn enough about technique to compensate for the lack of knowledge he brought to this job. "I couldn't have had a better guide than Cukor," he told Milne, "but I wasn't in the mood to learn."[36] He was, however, to be given another chance to work with Cukor, this time on *Her Cardboard Lover* in 1946.

After completion of *Sylvia Scarlett,* Collier was asked to write a film for Charles Laughton, who was to play a policeman. This time, Collier would be working with Irving Thalberg, the "Boy Wonder" who was the model for the movie mogul in F. Scott Fitzgerald's *The Last Tycoon.* As vice president and supervisor for production at MGM, Thalberg had turned that studio into Hollywood's most prestigious and glamorous, but he had suffered a heart attack in 1932. When he returned, much of his power was gone. Collier began work on the script, but Laughton left for England to star in *Rembrandt* for Vincent Korda. At the same time, Collier was offered a chance to work on *Elephant Boy* with Zoltan Korda, and Collier, too, left Hollywood for England. While he was in England, Thalberg died, and, in Collier's words, "all his slaves were put to death with their master and I was murdered in absentia."

Elephant Boy clearly was Collier's most amusing film experience. It began when Alexander Korda "rashly financed" Robert Flaherty "to make a documentary about elephants."[37] Flaherty, whose father was an iron miner and gold prospector, loved exploration and had already, in the teens of the century, produced a classic Eskimo documentary, *Nanook of the North.* He was more than happy to disappear into India and photograph elephants, but he did not bother taking the script, which apparently he had no intention of following. After some eighteen months, Collier was called in, since what Flaherty had produced was some 3,000 feet of miscellaneous photographs. As Collier told Milne, Flaherty was continuing "to make the most superb photographs of India, of the most ravishing temples, the most heavenly skies and particularly the most elephantine elephants, some of which were going to the right; others to the left; other seeming to charge directly at the audience."[38] To compound the organizational problem, the star, Sabu, was no longer so young as he had been at the beginning of the picture. In fact, his voice was changing. Collier was asked to create order from the chaos.

Collier took up residence in London, where for a time he occupied chambers in Gray's Inn. Money again became a problem. He moved to France, where he remained until shortly after the Munich agreement. Then, in 1939, foreseeing war, he stopped in Ireland and eventually returned to the United States, where he traveled extensively before settling again in Hollywood.

During much of his stay in Hollywood, Collier greatly enjoyed the extravagance of life, forgetting literature, he said, in order to indulge himself in the delights of existence; in terms of the dichotomy presented in *Gemini,* Valentine this time had temporarily mastered Orson. He recalled a series of jobs at Fox, Warners, RKO, Universal, Columbia, and MGM, which he remembered primarily as a series of gin-rummy games with delightful people. He was dazzled by the wit of the writers' tables and by the companionship of such figures as Marc Connelly and Dorothy Parker. He remembered Sunday badminton games with Harpo Marx and he best recalled having the use for six months of an estate belonging to Kitty Cox and her husband, Frank Vanderbilt, with its miles of flowerbeds and its peacocks that kept the guests awake.

For Collier, the tone greatly darkened during the McCarthy era, although he himself was never blacklisted. He met problems of two types. First, he was frequently confused with another John Collier, United States Commissioner on Indian Affairs, who was deeply involved with many causes, some of them perceived as leftist; the two Colliers are still confused in a number of indices and bibliographies. Second, a number of his friends were attacked. He was deeply sympathetic to their plight and to some of the causes they espoused, as well as highly indignant at the nature of the persecution. Although his own kind of artistic individuality precluded single-minded party commitment and although he found Karl Marx to be unreadable, he considered himself to be a sympathizer, and he found himself in an intolerable position. Deeply suspicious of all rigid ideologies, he nonetheless could not view a denial of party membership as anything but "truckling under" to the witch hunters in Washington and Hollywood.

Then, too, he was never fully comfortable in his role as scriptwriter. In his interview with Milne, he observed that what he wrote was probably too "literary" for the "glossy magazine thinking" of the times.[39] He had little respect for most of the producers and directors whom he met. "There are directors whose ego is like a raging lion looking for that which it may devour, and it usually devours the quality of the picture," Collier said in 1979. And such men are accompanied by "trained parasites" who write pictures to order, "vulgarizing and botching" as they go.

To their number, Collier refused to attach himself. His writing was slow, thoughtful, and painstaking, and his lack of speed was sometimes daunting to his colleagues. Paul Jarrico recalls an original screenplay, *Finding Ernie,* which Collier originally anticipated would take twelve weeks. A year later, he had written only 100 of the proposed 130 pages. "'John,'" Jarrico said, "'if it's taken you a year to write a hundred pages, how can you possibly expect to do the next thirty in two weeks?' 'Oh,' he replied, 'it's not the pages I haven't written that worry me. It's the pages I have written.'"[40] In *The Actor's Life,* Charlton Heston comments that Collier, working on the *War Lord* script, was "incredibly picayune on words and commas."[41] Collier's commitment to the accuracy and integrity of his writing was passionate and was sometimes passionately expressed.

Through the years, he became less active. In 1953, he went to Mexico City. On his return to the United States, he had an unpleasant confrontation with customs agents, and he realized that the FBI had amassed a file; being graylisted in this manner, he lost many profitable and interesting jobs. In 1955, he bought Domaine du Blanchissage in Grasse, France, and this remained his home until 1979. There he indulged his love for horticulture and the land, and he worked on his last major literary accomplishment, *Paradise Lost,* a filmscript that he was revising for the stage at the time of his death. He returned to the United States in the spring of 1979, settling first at Santa Monica and later in Pacific Palisades. He died on 6 April 1980.

Chapter Two
Paradise Lost

When Collier's *Paradise Lost* was published in 1973, novelist John Updike reacted with a roar of outrage.[1] Apparently upset by the notion of tampering with Milton's classic, Updike suggests that Collier's motivation must have been either the kind of money that Cecil B. DeMille gleaned from Exodus and Judges or the desire to create a literary curiosity. Christopher Isherwood came much nearer the point when he wrote that "even Collier's most devoted admirers will be astounded, as I was, by this masterpiece of his imagination."[2] However, in Collier's opinion, the Updike review ended all interest in the book, while the volume's ornate appearance, with its occasional, intrusive white-on-black pages, added credibility to the notion that this is a curiosity. Collier would have liked to see his script filmed and, when this proved impossible, began to adapt it for the stage, but he was not so naive or so avaricious as to be motivated by money. Neither did he intend to create a curiosity. His *Paradise Lost* was intended to sum up his own experience and much of modern man's.

Collier had come to view cinema very seriously. Milton chose the epic form because, at the time he wrote, that form was considered most distinguished; written superbly, an epic would have a weight and a force among literate men that could be achieved through no other literary form. Collier saw films as the most potentially powerful medium for communication in our culture, one with an appeal to an unprecedentedly mixed audience that includes the literate and the intellectual. That films rarely rise to distinction is not a fault of the medium itself but of the corporate structure and the devouring egos that govern the film industry. *Jaws* will be followed by *Jaws II,* not by *Paradise Lost,* nor is Satan's war with God a likely sequel to the *Godfather.* But serious work is both appropriate and possible; it is merely infrequent.

Unfortunately, his decision to modernize this particular classic and adapt it for the screen again led to critical problems. For some critics, there is something vaguely sacrilegious in either idea. With few exceptions, academic and literary critics still tend to regard film as an inferior genre, much as the novel itself was regarded in the nineteenth century. Collier was once again out of tune with his times, but deliberately so.

Under Collier's hands, the fall of man was to be recounted in a form accessible to a general audience. In a sense, he was repolishing certain aesthetic usages of the Middle Ages, not surprising in a writer who adapted figures from an early French romance for the personae of his poetry in *Gemini*. In an earlier age, the art of the stained-glass window and of miracle plays made the Christian story available to all, although only a small number of literate men could comprehend the complexities of theology; the rest were to be moved by the stories told by windows and plays, by the beauty of the glass, and by the humor, sometimes crude, of the drama. Further, Collier creates a tale that is to be read on several levels, much as the Bible and such works as the *Divine Comedy* must be read for literal, allegorical, moral, and anagogical meanings. Collier's version is an adventure story. It is also a psychological drama, depicting the forces that play havoc in man's mind. And it is also a vitalist drama.

On the literal level, Collier, from his long experience as a screenwriter, tells an adventure story, and there is no shortage of the common elements of adventure—blood, sex, war, temptation, terror. On a second level, he turns the fall of man into a psychological drama; his original subtitle was "Made into a Picture for the Mind's Eye," which would have emphasized this interpretation, and he was disappointed when the publisher turned this into "Screenplay for Cinema of the Mind." On the psychological level, the battle is between Apollonian and Dionysian forces—God, who represents the need for stability and for the status quo, and Satan, who represents the need for growth and creativity—in fact, between Orson and Valentine. Eve is a Demeter figure. It is tempting to interpret her as the synthesis in an Hegelian dialectic between thesis and antithesis, as Shaw might have written her, or as ego in the Freudian war of id and superego, but neither interpretation quite works. Instead, she is both the hero of this epic and a pawn in the games of power played between the masculine forces of heaven and hell. She is the life-giving, nurturing part of the mind, the female part, that is rejected by men but that is necessary for what Virginia Woolf termed the "fully fertilised" existence.[3] With Coleridge and Woolf, Collier apparently agreed that all great minds are androgynous.

Beyond this, Collier's *Paradise Lost* is the vision of a serious man looking back at his life. That life had spanned most of a century that had produced two world wars, a holocaust, and Vietnam. He sees the same archetypal elements that create havoc in the mind of the individual as those which have created chaos throughout human history. In a sense, he develops those archetypes in the images used by artists of his young manhood—the Sitwells, Diaghilev, Picasso—to depict these eternal conflicts, figures from the *commedia dell'arte*. If Collier's Adam is reminiscent of Orson, so also is he evocative of Pierrot, with Satan as an increasingly demoniac Harlequin, while Eve is the tragic, accidental *femme fatale,* the Columbine.

In his review of *Paradise Lost,* Updike complains that, since Collier is an atheist, his retelling lacks any central governing idea. Actually, what Collier says in his preface is that he does not believe in the Christian theology of Milton. In his writing itself, with its affirmation of life, energy, and creativity, there is evidence of another tradition, that of vitalism. Reverence for life itself is one assumption of this tradition, which was popularized early in this century by the translation into English of Henri Bergson's *Creative Evolution* and which underlies the work of such apparently diverse writers as Samuel Butler, George Bernard Shaw, Anäis Nin, and Colin Wilson. A second assumption, best stated by Bergson, is that such terms as good and evil, God and Satan, wrong and right, as well as the names we give ourselves and our concepts of time and space, are merely artificial structures that the human mind imposes on the universal flux. Such terms have no absolute value; they are simply intellectual conveniences.

In Collier's *Paradise Lost,* Adam and Eve, Satan and Raphael are seen as humans involved in a cosmic adventure story, but they are also portrayed as faintly stylized figures, acting out their inevitable drama, sometimes tragically and sometimes comically mortal and finite, against the immensely rich universe that is unknowable. At the end of Collier's tale, Adam and Eve are transformed into primitive cave people and evicted from the garden. Michael, whom they know only as the figure of God's vengeance, is then transformed into a guardian angel, smiling upon them although they are unaware of it, while Satan also smiles enigmatically. The cosmic order is something different and greater than man's knowledge of it.

In this cosmos, actions are evolutionary; one thing leads to another. For example, God's cruelty to the fallen angels, we are shown, will lead inevitably to the napalm victims of Vietnam. Similarly, the creative writer evolves from the writers of the past. At no point in his career did Collier question this; from *Gemini* through his literary borrowings in *Defy the Foul Fiend* and *His Monkey Wife,* he perceived the writer as craftsman standing on the shoulders of the giants. Even in his comic short stories, he plundered fairy tales and such authors as Theodore Dreiser in order to present his highly original notions within the stock forms and characterizations of his literary inheritance. In "Variation on a Theme," in fact, he mocks the extremes of literary types, those writers who are totally derivative and those at the opposite extreme who cultivate the myth of pure originality. It follows, then, that to tell the story of the fall of man, Collier would turn to John Milton's *Paradise Lost*.

His attitude toward Milton was ambivalent. "He's the only one," Collier said. "There's no other theme as great. It's the subject, the universal dichotomy between good and evil, the individual and the establishment." He did not believe, however, that Milton wrote a very good epic. All that most matters, he said, occurs in the first three books and at the end. He saw Milton's epic as badly constructed, and he theorized that the weaknesses in the later books reflect Milton's increasing blindness and a consequent failure of visual imagination. In *Just the Other Day,* Collier evidenced impatience with those critics who stressed the esoteric elements of *Ulysses* rather than its universal strengths, and he was similarly put off by the academic and theological speculation that attracts scholars to the later books of *Paradise Lost*. He was also put off by Milton's personality. He regarded Milton's "lip service" to the evil of Satan as evidence that Milton was "truckling" to the establishment, and he found the "woman business" in Milton to be "rather a bore."

What Collier wanted from Milton were the central figures, the "archetypes of human beings caught in the pregnant situations of the fable."[4] Where Milton had written brilliant lines that fit into Collier's own different construction, Collier borrowed these, usually not intact, either for the beauty of Milton's phrasing or to emphasize the continuity of history, just as Bernard Shaw borrowed the words of Christ for the heroine's moment of absolute despair in *Major Barbara*. Milton and Collier alike are merely conveyors of the fable.

Paradise Lost as Filmscript

Every age expresses its religion in the imagery most potent to that age. Milton, heir to the Elizabethan world view, sees heaven as a place of hierarchical order, and he describes the war in heaven as if it were an event in a Greek epic; literate men of his time would know those epics, and Renaissance warfare more closely resembled that of ancient times than it resembles that of the atomic age. Milton's battle was resolved with cannons, then among the most terrifying implements of destruction known. Such images were not helpful to Collier.

Instead, the technique of the film allows him to begin by depicting Satan's fall in images that terrify the modern mind. The initial scene is that of a pastoral and conventional Christmas card; the "blue night of infinite space" is illumined by a single star (3). As we watch, the star explodes. It becomes a comet. The comet disintegrates as the camera carries the audience toward it, moving us toward heaven's ramparts and then suddenly away again as a torrent of fire plunges from the ramparts into an abyss below, becoming the "rush of a hundred million falling bodies" (4). "Countless shouts of rage and screams of pain" "blend into a sound such as we have never heard before" (4–5). The single star and the conventional palaces and towers of heaven, first seen as in a golden sunset, are transformed into the chaos of a light and sound show.

The gold of heaven thus takes on new and ominous overtones. Gold, of course, is the traditional image of permanence; its imperviousness to rust and corruption has made it a symbol of what is sacred. In this scene, however, the golden torrent breaks into droplets, and in these bubbles appear the faces of mutilated angels, broken creatures falling into a lake of fire. This is the first association of the sacred color with the fires and flames of modern technological barbarity. Later, when Satan crosses the river Cocytus, the river of lamentation, he and his followers look into the water and see the ghastly recurrence of this warfare in history, so that man's history is a "symphony of sorrow," its musical instruments ranging "from the piercing shriek of a single napalmed child to the muted dirge of the hundreds marching to the gas chambers at Buchenwald, to the desperate clamour of the multitudes blinded on the outskirts of Hiroshima" (41). Again, Michael's sword resembles "an electric arc of immensely high voltage," and when he drives Adam and Eve from Eden he uses this sword as if it were a "cattle prod" (143–44). And an "electronic barrier" surrounds the garden itself (80). No word of dialogue is used to reinforce this set of associations, nor is one needed.

The camera also intensifies the temptation of Eve. Collier is not content with the pictures that come down to us in stained glass or on parchment, poignant in their long history but not especially tantalizing to a modern eye. Eve is naive, but she is the hero of Collier's story, not merely a weak and foolish woman, and she must be corrupted by something significant. So Collier creates fruit of the jeweled textures that seduced a generation of children when Disney used them in the 1930s and 1940s with all the effectiveness of a glittering display at Tiffany's or Cartier's. The forbidden fruits glow like gems against an enameled foliage.

Likewise, the camera turns the moment of Eve's fall into a dazzling, surrealistic fantasy. Satan first transforms himself into a shimmering, milky-skinned serpent, extremely phallic and extremely beautiful. Ever "flushing with new colours," the serpent then dissolves "from its own pattern into the reticulated pattern of sun-spot and leaf-shadow on the forest floor and on the trunks of the trees" (123). These lights and shades in turn seem to take on the configuration of the snake, until "the whole world seems to be made of the slithering Serpent coils" (123). Finally, Satan coils around the tree and becomes the tree. As he melts into it, the tree takes on his light and bronze and gold colors, rippling as if it had muscles.

Cinematic techniques also illumine the several layers of meaning. This is most striking in Collier's portrayal of Satan and his followers. On the simplest, most literal level, Satan's followers are the conventional demons: Beelzebub, prince of devils; Moloch, the Ammonite god who receives human sacrifices; Thammuz, associated with Adonis; and others. These serve as warriors, but they also represent psychological traits. When Satan's conquest of Eve is almost complete, he is tempted to back away from that action. At this point, his warriors become tempters, pointing out that, if Satan resigns his conquest, he must give up Moloch (wrath), Belial (hate), and Isis (pride). Visually, these figures are then to be seen superimposed on Satan's own face, so that it is clear they are various facets of his own personality.

At the end, the camera is used to stress the vitalistic nature of the story, pointing to an evolution that is not necessarily, and perhaps not ever, synonymous with progress. Adam and Eve, as they leave the garden, unknowingly pass the giant legs of Michael and of Satan, the humans now seen as midgets beneath the forces by which they have been overwhelmed and of which they are now unconscious. As they pass these titanic figures, the camera transforms Adam and Eve. No longer perfect, they suddenly possess the heavy brows and coarse features of earliest man as they shamble clumsily "out into the hostile world" to begin their evolutionary climb (144).

God

In his introduction to *Paradise Lost,* Collier writes that he has deliberately avoided portraying heaven for fear of the calendar art that inevitably results. He also has avoided any direct depiction of God. His refusal to show either is not solely a result of good taste. The world view that permeates this script does not permit any kind of simplistic portrayal.

Collier's cosmos, first of all, is a force, not a personality. Only a few vitalist writers have chosen to reduce the cosmos to the dimensions of their minds: Samuel Butler, for example, was convinced that all life exists within what is literally the body of God. We make up God's body, and that body, in turn, is probably part of the body of some greater God. Generally, however, such writers are less specific as was Bernard Shaw when he posited a "driving force" which is a "will-to-live, and to live . . . more abundantly."[5]

What appears in this script is not the force, if any, that controls actual life and change but Western man's reduction of that force to the God of the Judaic and Christian traditions, and this God, in Collier's eyes, is merely power run amok. Drunk with his own power, this God introduces violence, torture, and barbarity into the universe, and his followers throughout history have been quick to imitate his exploits. He also is the ultimate bureaucrat, dedicating himself to maintenance of the status quo.

As bureaucrat, it is necessary for him to have an administrative staff, and this staff provides the comedy in the drama. Raphael dines with Adam with all the arrogance of a Roman consul, but he lectures Adam with the tones and gestures of a ridiculously pedantic English schoolmaster, shaking his finger at Adam and sniffing at Eve as if she were something distasteful, like faintly rotting meat. Uriel, his classically flawless face "unmarred by the stresses of thought or sorrow or experience," is a good-natured dolt who is easily duped by Satan (55). Gabriel is a well-bred field marshal, absolutely virtuous and obedient. He is also witlessly unimaginative, so much so that he actually releases Satan on his own parole, assuming that the entire universe plays at the game of war as would a British gentleman from the playing fields of Eton. Michael, with his cattle prod, is a titanic rancher, although his transformation into guardian angel at the end of the drama shows how amorphous these personalities are and how much they depend on the limitations of the human imagination, not on what really exists in the universe.

Yet, even if these are human constructs and even if some of them are funny, God as conventionally conceived is a "monstrous inconsistency between infinite goodness and unbounded vindictiveness . . ." (xi). His vindictiveness is manifest in his decision to torment Satan's angels so that the youngest and most vulnerable are most grievously wounded. It is further evidenced in his condemnation of all of these to eternal damnation and infinite torture. It is apparent in God's invention of death, which exists long before Eve's fall. When Adam and Eve are first seen, they are raking up nuts, the life that is unneeded, and in this opening scene Eve already is mourning the waste. A similar scene occurs again near the end of the play. Adam and Eve will not, apparently, take life, since their hut contains no animal skin, but God will and has ordered them to rake up the seeds. There is vindictiveness, too, in God's treatment of Adam and Eve. An omnipotent deity casts blame upon Eve for what has happened, and, although his voice in the garden expresses compassion, he will not be moved from his death sentence, even when Adam pleads extenuating circumstances and Eve passionately pleads for Adam's life.

In his role as tyrant and bureaucrat, God thus stands for the desire for stability and the fear of change. God has created perfection, and, in Collier's words, "Perfection imprisons its possessor as in a crystal . . ." (xi). Permanence, and especially a permanence of middle-class creature comforts, is always Collier's vision of hell, just as it is Shaw's in the "Don Juan in Hell" scene of *Man and Superman.* But God has nothing else to do, once his administrative staff is in place, except to pack heaven with millions of what Uriel describes as songbirds, all singing hymns to the glory of their creator.

If this portrayal of God seems to resemble that of the devouring egos of Hollywood, this is not altogether coincidental. What Collier describes is the almost inevitable result of unleashed power at any level. First, there is the insistence on the status quo. Then there is the irresistible temptation to continue exerting power merely for its own sake. What follows is the kind of cat-and-mouse game portrayed here. In creating Eve, God has fashioned a being of imagination and dreams whose curiosity will inevitably lead to her fall. Warning Eve would do no good, but God, in fact, does not even warn Eve. He chooses to warn Adam, "not only because God takes no cognisance of the female, but also for a more extraordinary reason: knowing that Adam will fall, God does not wish him to have any excuse" (xi). A passionate defender of the oppressed, Collier reacts against the conventional view of Adam and Eve, pointing out that it is God who has defined the crime, created the criminals, incited the criminals to act, and then passed sentence on their actions. Collier's indignation, of course, is directed at those who believe that this vision of God represents infinite wisdom and infinite goodness.

Satan

If God's world is essentially a bell jar, Satan is the "virus" that invades the jar and causes its contents to rebel and to evolve (xii). To Collier, Satan's behavior is heroic. He represents the rebel against any establishment, as well as any underdog, and in his introduction of magic into the universe he represents the creative artist or the individual's creative impulse at war with the status quo. But, just as the power of the establishment can run riot, so creativity and magic are not purely benign forces. Thus, Satan appears here in three guises. He is the magus. He is sympathetic to life and comprehending of pain in ways that God is not. But he is overwhelmed, also, by the spites and vanities and arrogance that can accompany the creative urge.

Throughout the script, he is the magician. At the beginning, he pulls his followers from the lake of fire, and so great is his power that his own wounds and theirs heal before our eyes. Among these followers is Mulciber or Vulcan. He has joined Satan's ranks because, in heaven, he was forced to build all things according to God's specifications, and he longs to test his own creative powers. Using as his building materials his own thoughts, heart, and intellect, Mulciber creates the hall of Pandemonium. The camera superimposes the creation upon the body of the creator, so that he seems to become transparent, his body filling with an army of tiny laborers. All that he is, he uses, and so he dies when his creation is complete. At this point, Satan quotes Milton: "The mind is its own place, and/in itself can make a Heaven of/Hell, a Hell of Heaven" (20).[6] This is Satan speaking for himself, for Mulciber is but an aspect of Satan's personality. In like manner, the magician is evidenced by Satan's various disguises, especially the several transformations into serpent and tree during the temptation scene in the garden.

His emotions range from great pride to great compassion. Smiling and exultant as he raises his angels from the fiery lake, his mood changes when he sees the mutilation of the youngest angels. He weeps. At this point, he is described as courageous, sensitive, gentle, sweet, and understanding. But his very sensitivity causes him to be easily infected by the vices inherent in creation. At the Phlegethon River, Moloch is bitten by wrath, and so eventually Satan reacts wrathfully to Eve when she turns from him instinctively to meet Adam's needs. Beelzebub, crossing the Cocytus and hearing the victims of countless future wars, suddenly develops "that look of intellectual detachment common to those who advise the murderers of mankind" (41). Later, with similar objectivity, Satan stands back and observes the ruin of the garden idyll and of the woman he professes to love. At the Cocytus, also, Astoreth and Thammuz are sexually excited by the screams of girls raped in Dionysian orgies; after that, Satan lusts for Eve, and, like Samuel Richardson's Lovelace, longs to taste a woman's tears.

Upon the party's return to hell, all that has been experienced becomes part of Satan through the advisers who are aspects of his temperament. Satan, who had dreamed of forgetting Eve's temptation and, instead, making her empress of hell, repudiates his love for her. His is the proud and selfish love of the creative personality.

At the same time, like Adam and Eve, Satan is victim of forces he cannot control. He is the mate of Sin, he is told, but he does not even recognize her. He is the father of Death, but he is even ignorant of Death's birth. Permanently alienated and maligned, he is heroic because he intransigently asserts his own spirit against an unjust order, regardless of consequences and of the hopelessness of his struggle. But he is not the hero of *Paradise Lost* because he is not, in Collier's eyes, the person who performs the essential action of the story.

Eve

Eve is the hero. Lacking God's power and Satan's pride, she behaves spontaneously and autonomously, realizing fully her love for all that lives. She represents the female principle as the nineteenth-century anthropologist Bachofen and the twentieth-century feminist Woolf believed that principle to exist. Eve's strong desire to nurture and her love for life, her imagination and her practical common sense are qualities that Collier embodied in his heroines as early as *His Monkey Wife,* although Collier claimed he did not fully realize the humanizing power of women until he married Harriet Hess Collier. Whatever his conscious recognition, in his writings he expressed awareness of this power.

He also recognized it to be repressed. Eve must transcend God, Satan, and Adam alike, and, as it turns out, she must also transcend her critics. So great is her pleasure in her newfound sexuality after the fall that Updike refers to her as a "drugged porn queen";[7] Collier deliberately chose to create her as a deeply sensual woman, as opposed to the coy figure of ecclesiastical paintings or the chastened domestic of Milton. She is brunette, her coloring contrasted with Adam's Aryan beauty, and she is described as the source "from which spring all the southern and eastern races; all the darks and the golds of Africa and Asia . . ." (63). Her passion is not purely sexual but represents a deep longing for all life and all experience.

Her relationship with God is such that she cannot help but question his creation and envision other possibilities. In the first scene in the garden, she already queries why seeds must die and be swept away; she has taught small animals to eat from her hand. She dreams, and when she cannot express her dreams, she makes the gestures of a mother cradling a baby in her arms. On the other hand, she is not merely a visionary. She sees reality with the hard practical eye of a peasant woman. When Raphael priggishly lectures Adam, she responds with the glance of a country woman who believes her husband is being abused, and she is deeply hurt when Raphael describes her beauty as merely skin deep and questions the value of the carnal love she represents. The very fact of her creation, as she points out to Adam, has forced her into the role of rebel; if she is incomplete, it is God who has made her so, and that God's messenger should condemn her for what God has made seems profoundly unjust to her simple and practical mind.

Nor can Eve come to terms with Satan. She is seduced by Satan although the act is not consummated. It is his physical presence, as much as the fruit of the tree, that awakens her to a sense of the potential of life, and the force of his creative power turns her from idle dreamer to visionary. Swept up by Satan in her dreams, she rises into the heavens and from there sees the earth fully. But her love of life leads her to a less selfish path than Satan's. It is Eve who knows that Sin and Death can also be seen as Love and Birth; she gives names to things as simply and compassionately as does Shaw's Eve in the first act of *Back to Methuselah*. She is even capable of pity for Satan. Yet she is a pawn in Satan's game as in God's. God condemns her for what she cannot help but be; Satan views her with the greedy eyes of a connoisseur of beauty, appreciating her love for life but seeing her femininity as something to be possessed and even tormented. Satan's pride is wounded when Eve turns away from him to Adam, and he resolves to ruin her. Once again, Eve is convicted of a crime the nature of which entirely eludes her. The inadvertent *femme fatale*, the Columbine, she is ignorant both of her impact and of her choices. Satan accuses her of an offense against "the worship of life and change" (121); she does not know that such an offense exists.

Adam is patriarchal, and from him, also, she meets with repression. From the first time they are seen together in the garden, Adam walks some paces ahead of Eve, calling back his orders and his wisdom over his shoulder. He is totally oblivious to her responses or lack of them. His language is that of domestic comedy, expressing chauvinistic superiority when Eve tries to relate her dreams or to question the nature of existence in the garden. When Adam warns Eve to stay away from the forbidden fruit, he is the morally superior husband, explaining that he knows best what will lead to her happiness. He is also singularly literal-minded. Eve remarks that she has been hurt by Raphael's slurs. He uncomprehendingly asks how she can be hurt when no one has touched her. Dreams are the product of "disordered fancy," he tells her (119), and he cannot resist lecturing her on such matters in a dreary, "superior, puritanical tone" (118). Eve is not so much imprisoned or trapped by Adam as by her love for him. She does not repent of her fall until she realizes that Adam has rejected her.

At that point, she experiences a moment of absolute despair. When she sees Adam's misery in the face of God's sentence of death, she reacts madly, "like a mother who sees her child being tortured" (141). Weeping, she pleads with God for Adam's life, but God has gone. She is speaking to empty air. Comprehending, suddenly, the magnitude of the universe's injustices, she collapses and screams with pain. But the vitality that runs through her renews her. When Adam turns back to her, she is prepared to leave the garden, still maintaining the stubborn integrity and love of life that caused her to succumb to temptation. As they leave the garden, Adam shows her the axe he has prepared. Like Shaw's Adam, this figure who shows off his toy is prepared to go into the wilderness as warrior and father of warriors—for instance, Cain. "Who kills most, lives most," he tells her. With far greater wisdom, she answers, "Who loves most lives most, Adam" (142).

Adam

Adam is a rustic gentleman, a chauvinist, a farmer, a literalist, and "a paragon of all the deadlier virtues" (xiii). He is capable of rising to a single moment of heroic action when, rather than abandon Eve, he also eats of the fruit, but even then he manages to rationalize the matter to himself by convincing himself that God will not really exact the threatened punishment. To God he gives blind obedience; to Eve he gives lectures, and he is comically unaware that Satan even exists. As Eve eats the fruit and the course of human history is forever changed, Adam is seen "still delving" (123).

During their last moments in the garden, Adam resembles both the Adam of Shaw's *Back to Methuselah* and the Britannus of Shaw's *Caesar and Cleopatra*. Like Shaw's Adam, Collier's will become a killer and will breed a race of killers, but it is sadly evident that he and his dull-witted seed will provide the cannon fodder for anyone among them who proves to be a slightly more cunning homicide than the rest; his is the mentality that provides the troops to lead the prisoners to the ovens at Buchenwald. Like

Shaw's Britannus, he cannot deal with anything other than rules and regulations, and he is helpless in the face of his need to express emotion. Turning to Eve as he waits for the wrath of God that he hopes will never come, he attempts to speak of his love for her, but when he finally finds words, "the mountain of emotion gives birth to a spiteful little mouse" (138). He reproves Eve, wishing he had held her helplessly captive. As Eve regards him with compassion nonetheless, he finds a kind of strength by clutching at her like a frightened baby. His last lines are the marriage vow. He makes it quite clear that now they are bound together, for better or worse, until death. In answer to these words of an embryonic bureaucrat, Eve simply responds with praise. She speaks of the joy of being with him, and she speaks of gladness. These words, clearly, are not part of Adam's vocabulary. Eve will go into the wilderness to pass life on. Adam will go to find new kinds of structures, institutions, organizations, and ideologies to substitute for the sense of security that he has lost in leaving the garden. He is a child.

Chapter Three
His Monkey Wife

While there is considerable difference between the mature and tragic vision and the pyrotechnic visual effects of *Paradise Lost* and the themes and styles of John Collier's three early novels, the ideas that preoccupied Collier near the end of his long life are foreshadowed in the early fiction. *His Monkey Wife* is concerned with sex roles and with the relationship between the sexes, as well as with the satirization of London intellectual and fashionable society. Emily, chimpanzee heroine of the novel, is a self-actualized, self-educated, and humane force within a bestially human world and is, in short, a comic version of his later Eve.

Literary Tradition

His Monkey Wife, a comic masterpiece, is perhaps the finest representation of a type of light satiric fantasy that reached the height of its popularity before World War I, although Virginia Woolf achieved her first generally popular success later with *Orlando*. After the 1920s, fantasies tended to be considerably more serious in purpose and in tone.

The type probably had its English origin in Lewis Carroll's *Alice in Wonderland* (1865) and *Through the Looking-Glass* (1871). In *The Magic of Lewis Carroll*, John Fisher writes that Carroll, by 1850, had realized that he could convey in writing the same aura of magic that is produced in the public performances that enchant children with their peculiar blending of "mystery, suspense and tongue-in-cheek humour."[1] Following in Carroll's footsteps, G. K. Chesterton, Virginia Woolf, Max Beerbohm, and John Collier were also to practice this legerdemain. Of these, Collier was not only most successful but, adapting the technique to the short-story form, he also was able to repeat his success in an impressive number of works.

Apart from Collier's novel, the most lasting of the full-length fictions is probably G. K. Chesterton's *The Man Who Was Thursday*, subtitled *A Nightmare* (1908). Chesterton, a devout Roman Catholic caricatured by

his cape, swordstick, stomach, and mane of chestnut hair, had come to
maturity in the age of Oscar Wilde and the *Yellow Book*. The whimsicality
of that age is reflected in Chesterton's novel; despite its subtitle, this
nightmare bears little resemblance to the fantasies of the alienated Kafka
in the far different intellectual milieu of the Continent.

Chesterton claimed that he did not intend Sunday, the novel's central
figure, to represent God, but Sunday unmistakably resembles the
Jehovah of the Book of Job, with which Chesterton was obsessed.
Unquestionably, the plot is derived from Job with overtones of Francis
Thompson's "The Hound of Heaven." Gabriel Syme, a poet who is also a
Scotland Yard detective, attempts to destroy a vast revolutionary conspiracy. He is initiated into a Central Anarchist Council of seven members,
each of whom is identified by a different day of the week. Syme battles
these conspirators, only to find that each in turn is revealed to be another
Scotland Yard detective. Finally, Sunday, head of the Anarchist Council, is
also unmasked as the police chief, as well as the "Sabbath" and "the peace
of God."[2] After a number of complications, Sunday escapes with an
elephant and soars in the direction of heaven at the end of a balloon. As one
of Chesterton's biographers, Dudley Barker, has observed, it is as if
Chesterton were "commissioned by a publisher to write *Pilgrim's Progress*
in the style of *Pickwick Papers*."[3]

Max Beerbohm's fantasy, *Zuleika Dobson* (1911), was also a sensation in
its time, although today it is difficult to read with pleasure; it savors too
much of the private, inbred, aristocratic world of Oxford in the 1890s. Its
basic premise remains amusing. A great and charismatic beauty, having
risen from poverty to conquer Europe and the United States, now turns
her attention to Oxford. So well does she succeed that the students flee like
lemmings to the river, drowning for love of her. Zuleika was probably
modeled on Constance Collier,[4] but she might be drawn from the newspaper publicity of any of the great beauties from Lillie Langtry to Elizabeth
Taylor. At two points in *His Monkey Wife,* Collier may be borrowing from
this novel to hilarious effect: his chimpanzee heroine creates a Zuleika-like
sensation among the dusty scholars of the British Museum Reading Room
and among the passengers aboard a ship whom she approaches clad as
Carmen.

Virginia Woolf's *Orlando,* like *His Monkey Wife,* deals with matters of
sex. Like Collier, Woolf found fantasy to be the ideal vehicle for a light
examination of controversial issues; Woolf's book is a frank exploration of
androgyny, but fantasy permits such subjects to be examined without the
soul-searching and personal revelations that both authors would have

found embarrassing. Woolf's fantasy begins with a sixteen-year-old hero in the age of Queen Elizabeth I. At the end of the book, the hero has become a heroine, and the year is 1928. There is no real plot except English history itself. Scandal worked in *Orlando*'s favor, for the novel appeared only six days after the censorship hearing involving Radclyffe Hall's *The Well of Loneliness,* the first frank treatment of lesbianism. Woolf had been asked to testify at this hearing, and she had no doubts as to at least one reason for the success of her own novel. Writing to Victoria Sackville-West, her lover at one time and her model for the character of Orlando, Woolf observes: "The percentage of Lesbians is rising in the States, all because of you."[5]

Fantasies recur, of course, in later literature, but in such postwar works as George Orwell's *Animal Farm* (1945), fantasy is written with a heavier hand and sometimes a profoundly serious message and an air of self-importance. Nigel Dennis's 1955 *Cards of Identity* comes close to reviving the form, but without the sense of playfulness, while Flann O'Brien's 1967 *The Third Policeman* tends to lapse into a postmodernist obscurity, and Tolkien's Hobbits are morally earnest if they are anything. Bertrand Russell's short story "Satan in the Suburbs," the title story in a 1953 collection of his fiction, in many ways resembles Collier's fantasies of hell, but the heavy hand and wooden prose of the philosopher weigh the story down.

Collier's Plot

The figure of the monkey floats like a poltergeist through the popular culture of the 1920s. In 1925, the "Monkey Trial" of John T. Scopes in Tennessee attracted international attention, both because of the provincialism that it represented in its attack on the teaching of evolution and because of the quality of the legal adversaries, Clarence Darrow and William Jennings Bryan. In the mid-1920s, too, a Russian doctor residing in Paris, Serge Voronoff, offered to prolong youth by the grafting of monkey glands onto older men. Dr. Voronoff visited London in the spring of 1928, and his visit prompted a famous scientist to write to the *Daily News* saying that the monkey-gland treatment was dangerous because the characteristics of the ape would appear in the children of men who had undergone the treatment. This, in turn, was too much for Bernard Shaw, who was inspired to write a letter over the signature of Consul Junior, a performing chimp at the Regent's Park zoo. Consul Junior attacked humans in the name of chimpanzee integrity, arguing that it was not the apes who invented war, nor was the inquisition an invention of the chimpanzee. Let man do what he will, the chimp insisted; it is useless for men to use transplants to raise themselves to the respectability of the ape.[6]

Osbert Sitwell also involved himself. In a poem entitled "Subtlety of the Serpent" in his 1928 collection, *Out of the Flame,* Sitwell permits the serpent to comment on the superiority of monkey to man in that the monkey is ignorant of man's definitions of good and evil and of man's tendency to prefer, of the two, evil, but, above all, the monkey cannot attempt to conceal his moral or immoral actions through the falsities of speech.

Among the fashionable entertainments of the 1920s were costume dances, and, apparently, the eccentric Lord Berners, a member of a circle that included the Sitwells, at least once planned to attend a ball disguised as a monkey bride.[7] His biographer does not give the date; this event might have come as the result of Collier's novel. On the other hand, such a disguise would not have been surprising at any time from 1925 on, because fancy dress balls of all types were popular, and monkeys were, so to speak, in the air.

There are other possible sources for parts of Collier's plot. The 1920s produced a number of events that caused Collier and Lang in *Just the Other Day* to call into question the rationality of English marriage laws. They point to the plight of Mrs. Rutherford, who was unable to secure a divorce even when her husband, apparently a homicidal maniac, was sent to Broadmoor. The courts had satisfactory proof of murder, it seems, but for divorce much more than that was needed. The intransigence of marriage laws clearly is mocked in *His Monkey Wife* when Mr. Fatigay, the novel's hero, finds immediately after the ceremony that he has just been married to a chimp. He naturally consults the officiating clergyman, only to be told, "'Well, sir, what of that?'" The clergyman continues by saying that, since the latest scientific discoveries show the kinship of man and ape, it would seem that Fatigay has merely married a cousin. "'Marriage between cousins,'" he says, "'though I never encourage it myself, is perfectly legal.'"[8] The clergyman departs, leaving Mr. Fatigay to deal with his married life as best he can, having himself satisfied his bureaucratic soul. This is the kind of bureaucratic mind that Collier, much later, mocks in the person of Adam in *Paradise Lost.*

In *Just the Other Day,* also, Collier and Lang cite with near horror the case of Sir Leslie Ivor Victor Gauntlett Bligh Barker, who, despite his impressive name and masculine credentials, turned out to be a rather large woman named Lilias Arkell-Smith. The wonder, of course, is not that a disguised woman managed to court and marry another woman, but that the marriage continued for some years without the wife being the wiser. Only years later when the "husband" was arrested did his sex become known. This case was cited by D. H. Lawrence in his preface to *Lady Chatterley's Lover* as evidence of almost criminal ignorance on the part of English young people. Collier and Lang cite both the case and Lawrence's mention of it. Their sympathies are clearly with Lawrence, and, indeed, Emily, the chimp, with her natural sexual instinct governed only by reason and by love, is repeatedly contrasted with the inhibitions and related perversions of the fashionable English young.

These events and perceptions may have provided the starting point for Collier's quite simple story, which begins in the heart of Africa, moves to London, and ends again in Africa. Like any picaresque hero of an eighteenth-century novel or like Dickens's Pip in *Great Expectations,* Mr. Fatigay does not originally perceive the country to be edenic. Only after he encounters the corruptions of London does he voluntarily retire to Africa with his monkey bride. This follows a typical Collier pattern. Collier does not share Dickens's sentimental view of the country, but he is preoccupied with the vision of a lost Eden. It is lost. Only in a fantasy such as this novel can it be regained, but, under even the worst of circumstances, it is more likely to be approximated in the country than in the squalor and filth of a modern city.

Alfred Fatigay begins the story as a teacher in Boboma. Actually, he is merely waiting for his two years of servitude to end so that he can return to England and marry his fashionable fiancée, Amy Flint. Not a very intelligent man, Fatigay does not know that his pet chimpanzee, Emily, has proven also to be his best pupil, motivated in her studies by her love for him. While she has no power of speech, she has taught herself to read and has given herself a thorough, if somewhat uneven, education.

At the end of Fatigay's term, he indeed returns to London. Foolishly, he takes Emily, hoping that Emily and Amy will be friends. Emily does not expect much, having secretly read Amy's letters, but the situation is worse than she anticipates. Emily is forced to play Cinderella to Amy's wicked stepmother. She serves as Amy's maid, meekly takes abuse, yearns after Fatigay, and, when she can, climbs down a pipe so that she can improve her mind at the British Museum. In the meantime, Amy forces Fatigay into fashionable society, where she alternately flirts with him and pushes him away, desirous of his courtship but too selfish for any greater intimacy.

Believing Amy to be manifesting virtue, not selfishness, Fatigay remains eager to marry her. Finally, when the date is set and Fatigay has learned nothing from his experiences, Emily steps in. Menacing Amy with a knife, Emily forces the human to serve as bridal attendant while she herself takes the bride's veil. After the service, Fatigay learns what he has done, and, when the clergyman offers no help, he flees. Amy returns to her friends. Emily, stranded in a strange city, is forced to earn a living as is, in fact, Fatigay. The latter's schemes fail. He is reduced to selling matches, unsuccessfully, on street corners. Emily's infinitely greater practical wisdom leads her to become a star, almost immediately, on the London stage. She rescues Fatigay and restores him to health, confessing to him her deception just in time to prevent Amy from reclaiming him. Together, Fatigay and Emily return to Africa.

The Characters

Emily. Emily and her great contemporary, Bernard Shaw's St. Joan, may be the only two completely rational and sensible heroines in twentieth-century literary history. Just as Swift's Houyhnhnms represent common or horse sense, Emily represents rational behavior uncorrupted by the trappings of civilization. Within this novel, she is the only being capable of making delicate ethical decisions. In addition, she possesses a deep and natural sensuality, a hunger for knowledge, a generous nature, and a practical ability to cut ruthlessly through the frivolities and nonsense of ritualized social behavior.

Her sexual passion may well be what first shocked some critics. While Collier is no Lawrence and his treatment of sex is delicate, he establishes early in the novel that Emily's love for Fatigay is passionate, as well as maternal. In the early African scenes, Emily discovers Fatigay's correspondence and ruthlessly reads what she finds. Learning of Amy, she despairs and flings herself back into the jungle. She is about to allow herself to surrender to one of the most persistent and aggressive of her jungle admirers, Henry, when her common sense, not her prudery, tells her that nothing will be solved by this action. Quite pragmatically, she allows herself to be rescued from Henry's overeager attentions by holding his eye until a leopard has time to attack him. Again, Collier emphasizes her sexuality in the final scene of the novel. Fatigay and Emily have returned to Africa, but Emily remains reticent because Fatigay has yet to admit his love for her. He enters her room and sits on the edge of her "little white couch, wherein she sat upright, dark and dainty as a Spanish princess" (223). As he finally tells her of his love, Emily, ever efficient, reaches out a "prehensile foot" and, with it, turns off the lights (223).

Her sexuality is defined by contrast with two other characters, Loblulya and Amy Flint, who act out the extremes of passion and frigidity. The former, an aging tribal belle of Boboma, is the first to appear but is soon executed. Her lust is uncontrolled, and her fellow tribesmen, made aware of the extremes of behavior to which it will lead her, sensibly realize that her continued existence is a threat to communal living. Amy, at the opposite extreme, perversely transforms sex into a lust for power and into hypocrisy, as do her female friends. Regardless of whether these women profess virtue, modernism, or feminism, the latter another of the ideologies of which Collier was suspicious, all use language to conceal selfishness and self-indulgence in ways reminiscent of the monkey in Osbert Sitwell's poem.

Loblulya first appears. She has survived three husbands, all of whom headed their tribe and died of mysterious ailments. Her fourth husband has taken to the woods, having conveniently been advised by a spirit to absent himself from the village and Loblulya. Upon his departure, the tribe is suddenly afflicted with a strange demon who assaults, in ways that are not described, young men who walk alone in the jungle; the disappearance of the demon oddly coincides with the aging of Loblulya and her loss of speed. Still starved, she attempts the virtue of Mr. Fatigay, who, slow as he is, recognizes that he has a problem. It is Emily, however, who is quick-witted enough to protect Fatigay when the frustrated Loblulya vengefully screams that Fatigay is trying to rape her.

She is replaced by Amy Flint, whose Dickensian name, of course, reveals her character. Amy flirts with Fatigay and lures him, but, when he attempts to touch her, she screams that he is a sensual beast. Fatigay guiltily backs away, and the ritual is ready to begin again. She is made to seem representative of her time:

It is extremely difficult for a tenderly nurtured young woman of our race and generation, especially one who is diligent in keeping abreast of contemporary science, to say in so many words, "I like nothing more than being wooed, and nothing less than the prospect of being won," and this must be the reason that so few say it, while so many evince that attitude very clearly in their behavior. Not, indeed, that this is true of every woman, or that there is really a lack of healthy physical instinct among the cultivated shes of today. On the contrary, there is ample sufficiency, the only trifling criticism to be advanced being connected with the distribution of it, for half, like Amy, have none at all, and the other half have perhaps twice too much. (81)

What causes Emily to intercede to prevent the marriage is her realization that Amy will not change after her marriage. She has no warmth to share.

Unlike these other women, Emily is also characterized by a hunger for knowledge, an instinct much like that of Collier's Eve. Her intelligence has never been discovered merely because, according to the author, chimp intelligence has been measured by all the wrong tests. Like Einstein, Emily is not apt to go to a great deal of trouble if she is merely to be rewarded with bananas. Wisdom, however, is another matter.

Her early education takes place in Fatigay's schoolroom, where she learns the alphabet and nursery rhymes, bringing a highly original mind to bear upon this unlikely material. She perceives, for example, the lamb in "Mary Had a Little Lamb" as a tragic figure of unrequited love. She is deeply touched by the story of the Sleeping Beauty and Prince Charming, although her illusions about Fatigay as Prince Charming are shattered when he cures her of her romantic swoon by having her dragged by her feet from the classroom and drenched with water.

Matured by her experience, she moves on to more sophisticated reading which includes a thorough grounding in the best feminist thought of her age. She reads Charlotte Brontë, familiarizes herself with the works of Virginia Woolf, and, at one dark moment, takes solace in thinking of the sufferings of a suffragette heroine, "the divine Pankhurst" (97). She has studied the advanced thought of Bernard Shaw; she reads Conrad on the boat to England, discovering that he is far too fine a writer to be shared with her human fellow passengers, and her first act in the British Museum is to seek out Darwin's *Origin of Species*. Unfortunately, Fatigay's library contains a great deal of romance, and she is also familiar with Michael Arlen and the Georgian poets. She frequently quotes Tennyson, finding her own experience reflected in the Locksley Hall poems. Pondering Fatigay's treatment of her, she finds it all too true that woman is regarded as "something better than his dog, a little dearer than his horse!" (25).

Combining her own jungle experience and her reading, she creates her own highly original and autonomous moral code:

Emily considered herself to be as modern, in the worthier sense, as any of her sex, and though she deprecated the way in which many of her contemporaries appeared to fling away all regard for graciousness and responsibility, and even for the true development of their lives, in order to loot and ravage a few masculine privileges, she was capable, as in the case of Loblulya and of her sane benevolence towards Henry, of acting with complete decisiveness and freedom whenever she felt it to be genuinely necessary. (53)

Since she has just been responsible for Loblulya's execution and for Henry's assault by the leopard, her strength of character must surely be unquestioned.

Aboard ship, it is obvious that Emily is superior to the English, not only in her education but in her taste and breeding. Sensitive to the feelings of others, she is repelled by the vulgar attention she receives when the passengers learn she is a chimp, not Fatigay's anthropologist wife. For the ship costume ball, Fatigay insensitively suggests that they go as organ grinder and monkey, although Emily had contemplated Tennyson's Elaine, Carmen, or Ruth amid the alien corn. Emily, trying to find excuses for Fatigay's behavior, attributes his suggestion to a subtle desire to ridicule the passengers, and she, humbling herself, dresses as the organ grinder's pet. That act is a failure, but she returns clad as Carmen. The passengers are dazzled by her southern beauty, and "Subalterns, civil servants, diamond smugglers, judges, motor salesmen, confidence men, all that well-tubbed clean-limbed throng advanced to do her homage" (67–68).

London is no different. In Amy's presence, Emily feels "like something out of *Uncle Tom's Cabin*" (73), but she stirs the British Museum scholars until, like Beerbohm's young men, they are lurking, waiting, and pursuing. She reminds at least one of them of his mother. Amy herself moves on the fringes of Bloomsbury and Chelsea, and, when she has a party, there are so many men who resemble women and so many women who look like men that no one is apt to be startled by a maid who looks like a chimpanzee. One of the guests is the lecherous Wagstaffe, promising author of *Pandarus, or the Future of Bloomsbury*. Wagstaffe intends to seduce Emily, who, as servant, is the traditional victim of upper-class lust, but Emily scorns and evades him. Wagstaffe has long ago learned that a few platitudes about Einstein and a few unintelligible sentences about modern art are sufficient for the seduction of most modern women, so he ends closeted with Amy, who is dazzled by his garbled rendering of some words from Shakespeare. Emily is horrified.

Emily approaches a new level of maturity when she decides to prevent the marriage. She contemplates murder. Clearly, she has no general objections to the act, but her fine moral sense tells her that, in this case, it would be wrong. Suicide, she decides, would be equally immoral. She compromises by taking Amy's place, making her intentions known by threatening Amy with a carving knife while presenting her with a copy of Poe's "Murders in the Rue Morgue."

After the ceremony and abandonment, Emily uses this new maturity, her wits, and her resilient strength to build a career as a dancer. Contented with humble beginnings, she starts out as an organ grinder's chimp. From there, she works her way to stardom, her muteness being a virtue with theatrical figures accustomed to prima donnas. She has attained an elegant home and a chauffeur-driven limousine when she spies Fatigay, destitute and ill, and takes his "ragged" and "verminous" head to her bosom (188).

Alfred Fatigay.   Fatigay is a literary descendant of Ernest Pontifex in Samuel Butler's *The Way of All Flesh*. Like Pontifex in Butler's autobiographical novel, Fatigay has been educated as a gentleman and is therefore totally unfit for useful employment. Like Pontifex and like the English generation attacked by D. H. Lawrence, he also has been unfitted for life as a man. His sexuality is something he can neither acknowledge, condone, nor manage with any semblance of grace.

Butler and his protagonist were graduates of Cambridge, while Fatigay is a graduate of the less prestigious London University, but their education is similar in being bookish, rigid, and impractical. So little does Fatigay know of business that he assumes dreamily that he can establish the basis for a fortune by selling matches on the street. Although he is owner of the library in which Emily browsed, he is totally incapable of relating literature to life. Emily, having read Du Maurier's *Trilby,* imagines that Fatigay lived a bohemian student existence, but Fatigay's intellectual and aesthetic explorations seem to have gone no farther than Charing Cross Road bookstores. Indeed, his African students are taught to chant the motto "Character rather than Intelligence!" (56).

Just as Fatigay brings a set of literary conventions borrowed from Samuel Smiles and Horatio Alger to his life as a match vendor, so he brings a set of rigid cultural conventions to his life as a man. Females are either chaste or bestial. If they are chaste, they are virtuous, regardless of their relationships with the remainder of the deadly sins. Hence the cold Amy is a virgin to be adored, and he himself an evil creature for attempting to inflict his unfortunate male nature upon her.

Since Emily is, indeed, a beast, his relationship with her in Africa is that of a British empire-builder speaking to a native mistress, a fact of which Emily is painfully aware. Collier, at this point, adapts a passage from Virginia Woolf's *A Room of One's Own*. There, Woolf writes: "Women have served all these centuries as looking-glasses possessing the magic and delicious power of reflecting the figure of man at twice its natural size. Without that power probably the earth would still be swamp and jungle."[9] At nightfall in the jungle, Mr. Fatigay talks at Emily: "From simple allusions to physical fatigues and pleasures, he would proceed to higher matters, and would sometimes have daubed in a very fair self-portrait, rather larger than life, before an awareness of his reflection, gesticulating in the dark mirror-bright eye of the chimp, would bring him back to self-consciousness" (18). Emily has her limits, and she is not alarmed by the prospect of the world's remaining a jungle. She will only reflect Fatigay as he is. A New Woman if not a feminist ideologue, a student of Charlotte Brontë, she will bring Fatigay to heel as does Jane Eyre her Lord Rochester. Mutely but indomitably, she imposes her system of values upon him, since he has little system and few values that are genuinely his own. Throughout, she insists on her right to be treated as a generously loving, but autonomous, being.

Style

As in *Paradise Lost,* Collier sees art as polished craftsmanship, not as the simple and natural imitation of reality; in this first novel, he has developed the attitudes and techniques that will remain his until the end of his career. Already, he is as conscious as T. S. Eliot of being heir to a great tradition, but, like the Sitwells, he views that tradition without Eliot's ecclesiastical reverence. Collier was a playful and a witty man, and he enjoyed the comic possibilities of his inheritance.

Joseph Conrad is the first author to be introduced. As early as the opening paragraph, Collier warns his readers of the literary acrobatics that will follow, for much of the opening scene is a witty and delightful reversal of the first scene in Conrad's *Heart of Darkness.*

At the beginning of *Heart of Darkness,* a group of men is sitting on a cruising yawl anchored on the Thames. They include a company director, a lawyer, an accountant, Marlowe, who narrates much of Conrad's work, and the narrator of the first section of *Heart of Darkness.* The narrator looks at London and sees through the illusion of modern civilization back to the rich and barbaric substance of the past, "crowded with memories of men and ships" that the Thames has "borne to rest of home or to the battles of the sea."[10] Sir Francis Drake and Sir John Franklin come to mind, "the great knights-errant of the sea."[11] Suddenly, Marlowe looks even farther into the past and observes that "'this also . . . has been one of the dark places of the earth.'"[12] He speaks of the Roman settlements and the savagery of early times which holds for him "'the fascination of the abomination,'" with the "'longing to escape, the powerless disgust, the surrender, the hate.'"[13]

Collier begins with a reference to the "untidy tropics of this, the globe, and this, the heart" of the Upper Congo (15). But this jungle is an artifice, a stage set, in which trees lift their skirts so that we may see the props, much as "shopwindow ladies do, when their dresses are opened at back or placket, and we shall see only wire and emptiness" (15). In fact, each time we look in the jungle in this paragraph, we see a stage set and, through cleverly manipulated metaphors, we look through this set only to find another illusion. The jungle is a "highly colored Bargain Basement Toy Bazaar" (15), but the London set behind it is the set of a Christmas pantomime. The road into the jungle that, in Conrad's work, leads to that emblem of darkness Kurtz, here merely leads to the village hut of the obtuse Fatigay. In one sense, in Collier's vision, there is no dark place of the earth. In another sense, all alike are singularly dim.

The opening passage sets the tone for the novel, in which the social life of the jungle and that of civilized London are continually compared. While the jungle is not romanticized, it rarely suffers in the comparison. Amy and Emily both seek mates, but Emily's way is by far the more honorable of the two and even Loblulya's directness and simplicity are noteworthy by comparison with Amy's evasiveness. Henry, Emily's jungle suitor, pounces upon her as if she were some choice bit of food; so does the Bloomsbury author Wagstaffe, although Wagstaffe, unlike Henry, feels the need to conceal his motives by citing Einstein and misquoting Shakespeare, reminding the reader again of Osbert Sitwell's monkey in "Subtlety of the Serpent." The men of the jungle execute Loblulya as part of a male conspiracy against the female who makes life intolerable, but they do so without malice and without vulgarity. On the ship, Emily and her intellectual pretensions are mocked and savaged. In context, it is worth mentioning again that Emily, not the English, understands Conrad.

To stress these comparisons, Collier uses a series of metaphors reminiscent of Conrad's. Conrad's metaphors generally tend to take that which is exotic in the jungle and show its meaning by commonplace English comparisons. A native dressed and trained to serve as fireman on a boat is compared to a performing dog in breeches and a feathered hat, walking on his hind legs, and the approach to Kurtz is "beset by as many dangers as though he had been an enchanted princess sleeping in a fabulous castle." Members of the Eldorado Exploring Expedition are likened to pilgrims on their way to a shrine.[14] Collier reverses this, so that the reader looks at the strangeness of the English in terms of the natural images of the jungle. Charing Cross Road bookbuyers look "like those dull and crippled water insects which resemble bits of old dry stick, which, again, are exactly like booklovers" and a policeman looks like a "huge dytiscus beetle" (93).

In addition to the echoes of Conrad, which include some passages not mentioned above, Collier uses a number of other authors and some parodies of literary style to create the deliberately artificial effect of his work. The most obvious parody is that of *fin-de-siècle* prose. After Amy's disastrous party, Fatigay escapes to the London streets in pursuit of Amy and some of her guests. Having caught out Amy and Wagstaffe, Fatigay, in retaliation, has allowed himself to be almost seduced by one of Amy's friends. Amy has walked in on this tableau, has again accused Fatigay of bestiality, and has walked out. Learning nothing from his experience, Fatigay has accepted his guilt, and he takes to the streets in the mood of a despairing Thomas De Quincey. There follows a parody of the more ornate romantic and *fin-de-siècle* prose, a sentence of 350 words, filled with images of color and decay and opium dreams, and totally undercut by comically incongruous references to beetles and steak and kidney pie. Just as De Quincey stalked the streets seeking "poisonous shades for the sake of their strange glamor," so Fatigay seeks out the "incredibly white and Beardsleyesque" faces of an all-night café where the patrons anticlimactically gobble eggs and bacon (142–46).

Elsewhere, the reader's awareness of artifice is maintained by continual introduction of literary names and works. Emily's reading of Tennyson introduces a series of citations of that poet, either in the text, as when Emily considers dressing for the costume ball as Elaine, the maid of Astolat, or in epigraphs at the beginning of chapters. Amy's name, indeed, is probably taken from the Locksley Hall poems. In "Locksley Hall" and "Locksley Hall Sixty Years After," of course, the narrator is a man revisiting the home of his youth and remembering his cousin Amy, who proved to be disloyal and shallow, abandoning him for a worldly marriage. That Amy and the Amy of *His Monkey Wife* are, indeed, quite similar. Likewise, Emily's reading of Charlotte Brontë suggests that her name might have been inspired by the Brontës, especially since Emily's attitudes resemble those of Jane Eyre and her wildness is evocative of Emily Brontë's.

Literary allusions are used, in conjunction with certain kinds of imagery, to humanize Emily. Emily learns from literature, but she does not parade her learning. Literary references involving her usually appear in the form of her musings about the relationship between literature and life or as passing quotations that illumine her thoughts. Her flaunting of the volume of Conrad aboard ship and her display to Amy of "The Murders in the Rue Morgue" are isolated incidents. As is the case of any genuinely learned individual, she feels no need to show off. To emphasize her real intellectual and moral strength, she is usually described in terms of human imagery. She stretches out her hand, not her paw, and her smile is considered charming, frank, tender, or bewitching. When she is described in animal imagery, it is to create sympathy and an increased awareness of her real vulnerability, as when, hurt by Fatigay's insensitivity, she is compared with Ibsen's wild duck (21). Neither does animal imagery surround the few African natives who appear in the story.

The denizens of London are a different matter. They do not read literature; they merely quote it. When Wagstaffe impresses Amy, he does so by scrambling the first line from Shakespeare's sonnet 116 with part of the famous speech by Polonius from *Hamlet*. Amy's seductive friend Bella confuses Conrad's heroes with those of the silent film. And these humans are repeatedly described in animal imagery. In one of Fatigay's frequent skirmishes with Amy, he emerges with "his tentacles all awry" (149), and, when he is rescued from the gutter by Emily, his head is infested by vermin and is more ragged than was Henry's head at the zoo that Emily recently visited. Bella compares Fatigay to a lion, although he himself believes that he is usually perceived as a bear (138). After the disastrous party, when Fatigay has finally tracked Amy and her friends to the all-night café, Amy describes Bella as one of a tribe of "divinely desirable little animals," while Fatigay, taken aback by her coolness, can do nothing but gape helplessly like "a dead codfish" (150). As noted earlier, English bookbuyers are compared with insects and a policeman with a beetle. Scholars at the British Museum are seen as a "lowing herd" that "wound slowly from the tearoom, and lumbered in clumsy haste . . . to their places in the Augean barton within" (106).

These patterns support the structure that Collier began building with his use of Conrad in the opening paragraph of the novel. The jungle exists everywhere. Africa is not much different from London. Its inhabitants are merely less verbal and, consequently, less hypocritical.

Chapter Four
Tom's A-Cold (Full Circle)

Tom's A-Cold, Collier's second and least successful novel, is not now
generally available. Although the book was highly praised when it first
appeared, it is now interesting primarily as a well-written representative of
a peculiar type of literature and because of its theme, power. This theme
continued to preoccupy Collier as is evidenced in his writing of *Paradise
Lost* some forty years later. Without forcing the comparison, it is possible
to see a relationship, also, between this story and the myth of the lost Eden
that fascinated Collier from *Gemini* through *Paradise Lost.* In *Tom's A-Cold,*
the hero, Harry, is a natural leader, a force of nature, spontaneously in tune
with the needs of his people in the way of a Shavian hero, although far more
naive. The earthly paradise that he might well have created is disrupted by
his brother Crab, a Machiavellian serpent in the garden. The comparison
ends there; the more complete comparison is between Crab and Harry, on
the one hand, and, on the other, the Valentine and Orson of *Gemini,* the
men of action and the men of thought.

Literary Tradition

A tradition of utopian literature was firmly established by the end of the
nineteenth century. It included such works as Edward Bellamy's *Looking
Backward* (1888) and William Morris's *News from Nowhere* (1891). Problems in defining this kind of literature led to the use of another term,
"antiutopian," a term used for novels about less than perfect or totally
flawed worlds. This literature is sometimes said to begin with Swift's
Gulliver's Travels and to include works such as Edward Bulwer Lytton's *The
Coming Race* and Samuel Butler's *Erewhon* and *Erewhon Revisited,* as well as
more modern works such as Aldous Huxley's *Brave New World* and George
Orwell's *1984.*

Related closely to "antiutopian" literature is a third kind of fiction. This
type is called "apocalyptic literature" by Elmer Davis in his 1934 review of

a number of these novels, including *Tom's A-Cold.* [1] Both Davis and
Samuel Hynes, who explores this literature at some length in his *Edwardian Turn of Mind,* trace apocalyptic literature to the 1870s and to G. T.
Chesney's *The Battle of Dorking.* If antiutopian literature is cautionary,
apocalyptic literature combines its warning with sensationalism of the
worst that could possibly happen, offering a far greater appeal to the
widely expanding reading public of the late-nineteenth century than did
the rather more intellectual, speculative utopian or antiutopian novel.

At first, apocalyptic literature reflected anxiety as to the future military
intentions of Prussia, whose unexpected strength had been startlingly
revealed in the 1870 defeat of France. Hynes also sees in it a conservative
reaction to the late-nineteenth-century reform movements, representing
"a growing awareness of England's isolation from continental alliances and
a conservative fear that radicals, by transferring power from the traditional
ruling classes to the lower classes, would weaken England's will to defend
herself." [2] During the Edwardian period, according to Hynes, such novels
tended to be Tory creations, designed to breed fear of change and of
resultant weakness, part of a cultural pattern that included General
Baden-Powell's Boy Scout movement. This movement was born of
Baden-Powell's horror at a national disaster depicted in an anonymous
pamphlet entitled *The Decline and Fall of the British Empire* (1905). [3]

The quantity of apocalyptic fiction increased, especially from 1900 on.
Titles include Erstine Childers's *The Riddle of the Sands* (1903), William Le
Queux's *The Invasion of 1910* (1906), H. G. Wells's *War in the Air* (1908),
W. Douglas Newton's *War* (1914), Saki's *When William Came* (1914),
Edward Shanks's *The People of the Ruins* (1920), Cicely Hamilton's *Lest Ye
Die* (1928), and Michael Arlen's *Man's Mortality* (1933). Readers were
eager to be frightened. Sales were high.

In most cases, the earliest of these books depict an England unprepared
to meet a threat from abroad, often from Germany. But, with the
discoveries of the Wright brothers, the literature of invasion gave way to a
literature of fear; the invention of the airplane destroyed England's traditional defense, her isolation as an island. With this came the conviction
that English civilization could not only be invaded but could be completely destroyed, a fear that had been cultivated by H. G. Wells in his
narratives of extraterrestrial invaders starting with his 1898 *War of the
Worlds.* In 1908, Wells turned to the destruction of civilization in *The War
in the Air, and Particularly How Mr. Bert Smallways Fared While It Lasted,*
which, according to Davis, led directly to Collier's writing in *Tom's
A-Cold.* In Wells's novel, a German attack on New York turns into a world

war, and Smallways, according to Norman and Jeanne Mackenzie, represents "the common man faced by the ghastly reality of doomsday, brought about because mankind "'had not the will to avert it.' . . ."[4] Smallways survives only to see all organized government destroyed and men living as peasants in the rubble. In 1913, Wells produced a similar work in *The World Set Free*. Here he portrays devastation so great that world government spontaneously arises to put a stop to it.

The decades between Wells and Collier offered events destined to intensify the terror—the First World War, the Russian Revolution, the English Great Strike of 1926, the rise of Hitler and Mussolini, and the universal financial crisis of the early 1930s. In 1931, British sailors at Invergordon mutinied over depression pay cuts; in 1932, United States ex-servicemen marched on Washington, to be ousted by troops led by General MacArthur. The failure of the League of Nations put a stop to Wells's optimism concerning world government.

It is natural that a large body of readers was attracted to this literature. Not surprisingly, recent technology and blue-collar discontent have served to enlarge its scope, until it has come to take two forms. Polished and given a politically or morally earnest tone, as in works by Orwell and Huxley, it is considered serious literature and generally called antiutopian, not apocalyptic fiction, the former being the more respectable of the terms. When Germans, Communists, scientists, or bureaucrats are replaced by giant spiders, blazing hotels, or blobs that eat Brooklyn, the literature spreads through popular culture until it has become the staple of television and film during the past decade. The one constant is the little man helplessly enmeshed in vast technologies, ideologies, or conspiracies. While extremely urbane and literate, *Tom's A-Cold* fits well into the first of these patterns.

The Ideas

In *Tom's A-Cold,* Collier is atypically serious; there are few flashes of the wit for which he is known. Only vaguely is he concerned with the causes of the destruction of English civilization, attributing that destruction to an excess of participatory democracy. Committees have multiplied and bureaucracy and its red tape increased so much as to produce chaos. With its government a shambles, the country is left vulnerable to war and revolution. Collier is not concerned with describing the ensuing battles. Rather, he deals with the aftermath, leaving himself free to explore the nature of power, the nature of heroism, and the proper relationship between a leader and his people.

In this story, he reveals the hard-headed realism and the consequent lack of faith in permanence and in lasting ideologies that later color his *Paradise Lost.* Humans are born as they are, just as Emily is born a chimp and Eve is born to dream. Make what they can of themselves, they are vulnerable to outside forces beyond their own control, to fatal flaws within themselves, and to forces of change that are inevitable. While Harry, hero of *Tom's A-Cold,* is born to be a hero, a glowing, golden figure reminiscent of King Arthur or Shakespeare's Prince Hal, his ultimate success is problematic. Harry's power of leadership may well reflect the influence of Nietzsche and Shaw, but his destiny is not assured. Shaw's heroes control their fates; Collier's Harry can only attempt to do so.

The problem of the novel, in which the characters spend a disproportionate amount of their time discussing power and leadership, is the problem of the relationship among the classes in the rebuilding of civilization. Collier takes the stance that there must be a revival of the natural alliance between workers and aristocrats, a stance much like that of Disraeli and his Young England movement in the nineteenth century. It is fundamentally a conservative position. Its assumption is that the natural aristocracy, unlike the middle classes, will govern responsibly, and it reveals great compassion for the underdog, the same compassion that is evidenced for Emily in *His Monkey Wife* and for Eve and Satan in *Paradise Lost.* With it, there is profound dislike for the greed of the middle classes, a hatred for acquisitiveness and possessiveness that informs all of Collier's works including the comic short stories and that is related to his distaste for the conventionally conceived, exploitative God in *Paradise Lost.*

For Collier, indeed, the bourgeois is always suspect. His most impassioned words appear in a brief essay entitled "Please Excuse Me, Comrade," written for a bibliography compiled by John Gawsworth for the second series of *Ten Contemporaries: Notes Toward Their Definitive Bibliography.* In that work, Gawsworth combines bibliographic descriptions of the early works of a number of writers considered promising at the beginning of the 1930s—Dorothy Richardson, Stella Benson, and Liam O'Flaherty, among others—with original, usually autobiographical sketches by these writers. What Collier contributed was an explanation of his retreat from London to the country. Viewing the population of London, he rejects middle-class values, those who aspire to them, and those who manipulate the poor by positing these values as ideals:

. . . to be perfectly frank, I have become so ill-natured, that, looking on their Press, their pylons, their picture-palaces, their politics, I no longer feel in earnest remonstrative mood, like a little self-constituted good shepherd . . . but I rub my hands, and say, "Hurry up, you foulers of a good world, and destroy yourselves faster. Flock to be clerks and counter-jumpers and factory hands. Eat your tinned food. Build yourselves more of the houses, reach-me-downs, faces, lives, which express your single soul so well. Read your newspapers: they will tell you you are all right, that you should breed. They would tell the rats so, if they grew up to be certified readers. Spoil every good thing that stands in the way of trade, and praise every ill thing that can be made and sold. . . . "[5]

He calls the English Gadarene swine, plunging to self-destruction, but he makes exceptions of those who maintain their individuality, from James Joyce to the country cottagers who still continue to do their work in good conscience.

The title of the essay alone indicates Collier's rejection of the leveling tendency of twentieth-century culture and politics. Although, for the time, he believed in the possibility of enlightened government by an aristocracy, he altered his beliefs through the years until he told Milne, in 1976, that he was then embarrassed by some of his earlier attitudes. For the period of this novel, however, he had placed himself rather toward the right of the political spectrum, allying himself with older and traditional writers such as the Sitwells, rather than with the younger generation of Auden and Spender.

The Plot

The year is 1995, and the setting is Hampshire. A "tradesman's world" has resulted in the destruction of civilization.[6] Survivors have returned to tribal existence, although a few old men including Harry's parent, simply called Father in the book, remain alive to pass down the best of the traditions and learning of the past and to warn the young against repeating the follies of the past by "cataloguing varieties of the baseness which Parliaments, county councils, village councils had drawn as it were out of the hearts of their constituents and accreted like cancers in the heart of the general life" (239).

Harry's tribe is not the only one, and each has found a different mode of existence. Thanks to Father and a dying squire named Tom Willoughby, Harry's clan retains the manners and language of the best classes of the

world that is gone. Bacon and Lamb and a few other writers are still
remembered, but so much is forgotten that Galen serves as a medical
handbook. Unfortunately, there are few who can read him.

Greed is not yet dead. While Harry's tribe dresses well, members must
disguise themselves in rags when they leave their community so that they
do not attract the attention of the less fortunate. They eat relatively well,
much in the manner of the Middle Ages. Their pigs are their greatest
treasures, but, again, they do not dare to raise many for fear of bringing
down marauders. Otherwise, they eat plovers, wood-pigeons, partridges,
squirrels, hedgehogs, snipe, wild ducks, small birds, and snails, and they
raise a few fowls, bees, and eels, as well as some fruits and vegetables. All
this is evidence of progress; when the wars and revolutions ended, the
survivors ate rats. But the community is still not strong enough to farm
freely without fear of its neighbors.

Head of the tribe is a man named Chief. Once, Father had been leader,
but he was shoved aside by this younger figure, who represents a return to
bourgeois values. Chief is both greedy and lazy, and, early in the book,
Harry catches him seducing a girl who is no more than a child, bribing her
with a trinket. Essentially, Chief has the mentality of a political party
hack. The concept of responsible leadership is beyond his comprehension,
and he sees no reason to worry about the constricted life of the tribe. He is
not an unpopular leader. Rather, he has the crude charisma effective in
modern elections, being described as "beautiful, coarse, genial, brutal,
shrewd, and stupid" (8).

Like many lazy and lecherous men, he is contemptuous of women. One
of the survivors of the world before the war is Lady Alicia Willoughby,
Tom's wife, a doctrinaire feminist. This woman has continued fighting her
private battle, based on "ego-feminism," long after wars and starvation
and the necessity for returning to a primitive division of labor have
rendered such rhetorical battles irrelevant (40). Her intrigues, in fact,
resulted in the rise of the chauvinist Chief. Chief vents "on the other
women that hatred which she had inspired in him, till in the end no
woman dared raise her voice in the general talk, and they sat apart at
mealtimes, and talked with their men only in private" (41).

The Chief's aide and logical successor is George, a sadistic hatchetman
whose first reported action is the injuring of a stranger who "went on
screaming for quite a while, George not troubling to finish him" (32). He
is repeatedly described as a wolf. George promises to be even a worse leader
than Chief. He is hostile to the entire tribe and is totally selfish. After a
raid on which the plot depends, George wants to take one of a group of
captured women, foisting his own aging wife on one of the younger men.

When this idea is opposed, George is enraged: "The terms by which he grasped life were in essence identical with the Chief's, except that they were darkened by the bitterness of his nature; his was a world of 'damned sermonising old men,' 'damned swollen-headed pups,' and 'women.' These objects had often enough proved refractory in a small way. . . . It was fantastic, a nightmare, that such furniture should openly rebel . . . " (188–89).

Opposed to Chief and George are Father, Harry, and Father's other son, Harry's half-brother, Crab. Crab is an intellectual, named after the hermit crab, and his body is crippled by rickets. As with the figures in *Gemini*, these two brothers are so close that Crab feels himself to be Harry's unconscious. Crab is a student of the power that he himself can never hold. He has read Machiavelli and perceives himself to be the advisor to a ruler. His behavior is considered, bookish, and shrewd until he is undermined by his own passions, of which he is only partly aware.

The action of the novel is triggered by the tribe's need for women. There are few, and the young men of the tribe are squabbling over them; there is also too much inbreeding. Chief knows of a place where women are "thick as lice" and where a "parcel" of them can be obtained (10).

Harry and Crab go scouting, and their expedition allows Collier to show other forms of tribal life. In depicting one such group, Collier borrows from Swift's Yahoos to portray a forest people who have so interbred as to produce a race of "prognathous jaws, ridged eyebrows, spindly legs and retreating foreheads" (69). A few of these atavists go naked; some wear dog skins around their loins, and the women can be distinguished solely "by their dugs and by the absence of the patchy, scrubby beards that the men wore" (68). They have forgotten whatever manners and language that their ancestors knew, grunting to each other and tearing their meat from a rancid stock. They mate in public. On the other hand, Harry and Crab also find a society that has re-created a medieval manor with fortress and farms, and, from that, Harry derives an idea of how the life of his own tribe could be made richer and more generous.

They decide to attack a relatively sophisticated tribe whose economy is based upon the fact that the knowledge of breeding sheep and of spinning has been passed down. Harry falls in love at first sight with a young woman whom he sees leaving the castle, so he insists that this place be raided. Since he has caught the Chief seducing the child, he can blackmail the Chief to get his own way.

Despite Chief's bungling, the raid succeeds under Harry's leadership. After a great battle, the men return with the captive women including Rose, the girl Harry loves. Under Father's supervision, the women are offered every courtesy in an attempt to make the best of a bad situation. They are doled out to the young men, and Harry, of course, receives the woman of his choice.

Wounded in the raid, Chief lies wallowing in self-pity. Crab was responsible for his injury; now Father and Crab decide to kill him so that Harry will lead the tribe. They do so, but blood begets blood as in the Shakespearean drama of which there are suggestions throughout; Shakespeare's *King Lear* gives the novel its title, and, from *Henry V,* Harry takes his character. Rose has left behind a brother with whom her ties are as close as those between Crab and Harry. The brother traces the girl and is killed by Crab, who recognizes the resemblance between this stranger and Rose. Jealous of Rose, he parades in the dead man's clothing. Rose realizes what has happened, escapes, returns to her own tribe, and leads a raid on her captors. She is responsible for the death of Crab and in turn is killed by George. Harry kills George and, in doing so, brings down upon himself the wrath of the tribe. While he mourns Rose and Crab, he is lectured by his father. At last, he returns to his men, presumably to assume his natural role as leader. His success is suggested but in no way assured when the novel ends.

Principal Characters

Harry.   Harry resembles Shaw's Caesar in his instinctive grasp of the powers and responsibilities of leadership. A natural aristocrat, he has been educated by Father to be contemptuous of Chief's sordid values. From childhood, he has known how to exert authority, never asking a favor of his elders "except when he had such authority behind him as would make refusal impossible" and never displaying authority "till it was challenged, so that those who would have refused him if it had not existed, had yet got into the habit of acceding to his bare word" (14). His personal magnetism is such that he alone is able to lead the raid, banding the young men of the tribe together to do what is necessary.

His attitude toward his fellow tribesmen is not the hostile and self-serving attitude of George, but Harry for his own reasons is impatient with the democratic processes that wrecked the older civilization. His own will and the advice of the tribe's elders, he asserts, will provide all the government that is needed, and he refuses either to make speeches or to answer questions in order to increase his popularity. In battle, Harry is willing to kill, but he, like Shaw's Caesar, will not tolerate murder for the sake of mere domestic or political manipulation, and he is ignorant of

Crab's plot against the Chief. When Crab urges Harry to connive for power, Harry points to the ruins of old England as the result of "ten thousand generations of murder" and asks: "Are we now to start the turn again? Here we are, back at Eden's gates; and who dares to strike Cain's blow and set us off on the old track once more?" Like Satan passing over the river of lamentation, he hears the voice of history as a host of shrieks and a "cataract of groans and gurgles!" (84). That he comes to power as a result of murder and that Crab's initial murder leads to a torrent of blood support Harry's hypothesis, although he is ignorant of the beginning of all this.

Like Caesar, he identifies his own good with that of the tribe, and in this he is correct. Father attempts to warn Crab away from interference, cautioning Crab that a leader like Harry is a "force of nature" and that he leads "by a force quite other than that which makes and moves us" (207). This is true. Harry sees the narrowness of tribal life and realizes that the young men need to be given a sense of direction, a goal, if they are to do men's work; this can only happen, he realizes, under his own direction. He confides to Rose his dream of building an estate such as the one he saw on his scouting trip and his pleasure in watching faces light up when he enters a room: "Selfishness, unselfishness: they mean nothing now. When I build myself the stronghold, all shall be sheltered; when I call for sheep, every man shall eat mutton and wear wool; when I seized you, I brought to everyone that loveliness that makes life worth living, light in our darkness, for we had none of it before" (214).

Unfortunately, Harry's fatal flaw is his sexual innocence. In the motherless world of his household and in a community governed by the chauvinistic Chief, he has had no chance to learn that a woman worthy of his love will have a personality of her own. His innocence causes him to treat Rose as a beautiful object and, like Adam, to address his mate as if she were a child. Twice, in fact, he addresses her as "child" at the precise time she is planning, after her brother's murder, to escape back to her own people (262, 263). He is completely oblivious to the ambivalence of her response to him and to the bonds that were important to her in the past. Like the funnier Edward Laxton of the short story "Sleeping Beauty," he even seems incapable of understanding that she had an existence before she came to him.

He adores her as a goddess and subdues her in the manner of a D. H. Lawrence hero. Rose ceases to struggle when Harry kidnaps her after she feels the power of his hand. A few of Collier's phrases, in fact, are strongly reminiscent of Lawrence's writing, as when he describes the trek back to the tribe after the raid: "When she felt his grasp, all her sense, all her curiosity, . . . life itself, flowed into her hand, leaving her body empty. . . . She felt, with all the relief of hopelessness, that she need try to scheme no more, it was too strong . . . " (175–76). Taken back to his tribe, she quickly perceives him as a god. She "quivered . . . and was his" (200).

This profound sexual attraction lasts, but Rose has other ties. Her brother is almost her twin, and with him she has lived a "Hansel and Gretel childhood amid the brutishness around them" (173). Collier takes great pains to emphasize the analogous relationships between, on the one hand, Harry and Crab, and, on the other, Rose and her brother, so as to give as much attention as possible to the degree of Harry's blindness. Harry recognizes the emotional potential of neither set of relationships. Even as Rose dies, calling out Harry's name, he is still asking her why she behaved as she did, still failing to comprehend the depth and complexity of her conflicting allegiances. Harry, the natural leader and man of action, lives in a world of simple decisions and judgments. Reality, unfortunately, is different from what he supposes.

Crab.   With his twisted body, lust for power, and distorted sexuality, Crab is one of Collier's most fascinating characters. He stands as evidence of Lawrence's attack on sexuality sublimated to the intellect.

Crab is the lone intellectual of the tribe. As the half-brother of Harry, has appointed himself grand vizier; he feels that "there is no happiness but in power," which he will enjoy through Harry (116). From the beginning, this Valentine figure has studied to be the complete Machiavellian, urging Harry to conspire when Harry's intuitions correctly advise him to act directly. Symbolically, on the scouting expedition, it is Crab who slithers through the underbrush, inch by inch, like a snake; Harry is too forceful for this kind of espionage. And there is a sense in which Crab is the snake in the garden envisioned by Harry. Crab is not a visionary, like the Satan of *Paradise Lost*. Lusting for power for its own sake, he is destructive.

There is also a strongly feminine element to his character. This fact is stressed throughout the novel, although Harry remains unconscious of the homosexual element in Crab's love. Harry's relationship with Crab is effective so long as Crab, who fancies himself to be Harry's unconscious, fills the role of the feminine side of Harry's personality; together, they are the androgynous whole. The relationship collapses with the advent of Rose. Envious of the girl, Crab reveals his jealousy to Father, saying, "I have too much of the woman in me, where Harry is concerned, and it nags at my heart" (205). Such words as these are repeated throughout the last hundred pages of the novel. Because Crab is jealous, he attempts to draw

Harry away from Rose. Made conscious of this, Rose resentfully makes a point of being even more flirtatious with Harry.

Crab's psychological reaction to any threat is to strike out at the world that has crippled and deformed him. His body contorted because of famine, he feels victimized, not realizing, as Collier would have the reader be aware, that we all are victims. From a hiding place, Crab wounds Chief, who at that point cannot defend himself. He then conspires with Father to contaminate the Chief's wound and next to kill the Chief. In doing so, Father acts against his own principles; Crab does not. Similarly, after one episode during which Rose, recognizing his jealousy, flirts with Harry, Crab storms out in fury, recognizes Rose's brother, and kills him simply as vengeance against the woman. Even knowing the probable consequences to himself, he cannot resist hurting Rose, so he parades at dinner in the dead brother's clothing. Having done his worst, he virtually collapses, feeling drained, so absolute is his surrender to his emotions. He stares at Harry, "drinking in his gaze, as woman repentant after some hysterical fury drinks in reassurance from her lover" (256). At that point, the final catastrophe is inevitable.

The Writing

The strengths of *Tom's A-Cold* lie in its descriptive passages, especially those dealing with landscape and battle, and in the development of Crab's character. The weaknesses involve the long discussions of the nature of power and leadership, although there is an additional problem with the undeveloped character of Rose.

Structurally, the book lacks balance. This is almost inevitable in utopian or antiutopian fiction; it is not merely a single writer's difficulty. If an author is to introduce his reader to a new world, then he must describe that world at some length. He cannot rely on those assumptions that a reader normally brings to works of fiction. Collier wants to return his modern readers to an England that in many ways has regressed to the rugged landscapes and great forests of early times but that in many ways is unique. He must illumine the nature and problems of Harry's tribe and show alternate ways of surviving. The result is that too much of the first five chapters is narrative description of landscape (much of it beautifully delineated), so that, when the principal characters are introduced, relatively little time can be spent in character development.

The problem is compounded by the fact that only Crab and Father have any great intellectual range, including the power to abstract, and so the principles of power, leadership, and class relationships that are at the heart of the book must be presented through discussions among a quite limited number of characters. In an effort to communicate his ideas, Collier must allow these characters to speak at rather great length.

Rose poses an additional problem. She is seen mainly through Harry's eyes, and Harry sees her only as a one-dimensional figure. Because of the nature of her difficulties, she cannot confide in her equals in terms of will and forcefulness, Crab and Father. Because the women of the tribe are totally repressed, she can have no woman confidante; this would be a normal mode of allowing a woman to air her grievances in fiction that adheres to more regular conventions. Consequently, when, late in the novel, it is time for Rose to flee and return to her people, the groundwork that would create comprehension of her action has been incompletely laid. Since the reader is intended to regard her with sympathy, the author must intervene and offer explanations.

At the same time, Crab is among Collier's most haunting creations. At various points in the story, he is sweet, tender, complex, passionate, thwarted, jealous, diabolical, and pathetic, and all convincingly. Because Crab is articulate, it is possible for the writer to develop fully, yet economically, the many facets of this character, so that even on the scouting trip early in the book the foundation is laid for all that Crab will later do. All that remains to be presented is the fascinating delineation of his gradual awakening to his own motivations.

Individual descriptive passages also are excellent, although the amount of description slows the story. Everywhere in the novel there is evidence of Collier's knowledge of the minutest detail of rural life and his profound love for the English countryside. He identifies fauna by specific name, where most writers would only speak of quantity and general type. There is also an awareness of subtlety of color and shade that, much later, is refined into the visual pyrotechnics of *Paradise Lost*. Typical of his description at its best is a passage showing the landscape as Harry and his men march to capture their women:

The moon at zenith silvered all, paling the stars, and showering its arched rays like the wires of a bird-cage. The trees on either side were flat and black against the cobalt fringes of the sky. The white owl floated along the edges of the glades; the summering snipe rose with its nothingy shriek from the shaggy moon-soaked ground at their feet, and the bittern woke and boomed in the untrodden marsh ahead. Against the trees their faces looked white, hollow and hard as bone, under their shallow helmets; against the pale sky they were sharp and dark as bronze. (136)

The painstaking eye for detail, of course, is typical of Collier in all his writing.

Collier's descriptions of violence also are effective. Often in his fiction he evokes, with startling and haunting effect, the sense of the violence that lies just below the surface of even the most mundane human relationships, especially domestic relationships. Here he does this and more. His scene of the battle that ensues when Harry and his men conduct their raid is vividly effective, reflecting his full appreciation of the art that went into the adventure tales that he enjoyed in his youth. Other kinds of violence are so arranged that they interrupt the most prosaic of activities; Collier captures the sense of abruptness and immediacy with which such events intrude into real life and the sense of shocked and stunned disbelief that afflicts the witnesses. Of his early writings, these scenes most clearly foreshadow his later career as a filmwriter.

Chapter Five
Defy the Foul Fiend

Collier's final novel was *Defy the Foul Fiend*. It is typical of Collier to reverse what is expected by publishing his most autobiographical work last. His hero, young Willoughby Corbo, is the same age as was Collier when he wrote the book. Corbo also has undergone an exceedingly bookish education, and he duplicates Collier's flight from urban sophistication to the life of a country squire. Caught up in his dreams of a lost Eden, he does not find paradise. Instead, he finds himself the victim of circumstances he cannot control, Bergsonian forces of time and change. Incidents in the novel are so submerged in comic exaggeration and in borrowings from other works of literature, however, that specific autobiographical elements are almost impossible to discern.

Literary Background

If Henry Fielding's *Tom Jones* and *Joseph Andrews* are termed picaresque, then Collier's *Defy the Foul Fiend* must be similarly categorized. The plot is loose, as in those eighteenth-century works, moving the hero from country to city and back to country again. While the same kind of plotting and the same kind of contrast between urban and rural values are found in such nineteenth-century works as Dickens's *Great Expectations,* Collier's crafted sentences, his sharp satire of everything, including his hero, and his unwillingness to sentimentalize anything, including his hero, heroine, and rustics, are more typical of the eighteenth-century fiction that he studied as a child than of the nineteenth century. Moreover, there is a trace of Voltaire's *Candide* in this novel, a foreshadowing of the eighteenth-century reconstruction of John Barth's *Sotweed Factor.* It is evident especially in the tone that the author takes toward his hero's wide-eyed optimism. Corbo's chronic inability to comprehend his world and his wide-eyed floundering about in that world are inevitable and they are comic; they are comic because the hero's errors are treated ruthlessly. It is clear that, in the eyes of the author, innocence of society's laws is not sufficient reason to absolve the culprit of guilt. As in the case of Candide, optimism is childish. And it is self-destructive.

A second literary term, the *Bildungsroman* or "novel of development," has come into use in recent years, partially replacing the term "picaresque," which was used in the early decades of this century. A *Bildungsroman* is tightly plotted, according to current definitions; a picaresque novel is not. Depending upon a given critic's definitions, this newer term can comprehend novels ranging from *Tom Jones* to Roth's *Portnoy's Complaint*. In these novels, the central character attempts to find his place in the world. He encounters problems and creates problems for himself, and, in the course of solving these problems, he matures. Often, Samuel Butler's *The Way of All Flesh* is called the ancestor of this school of writing; certainly, Butler's novel was enormously influential in the early decades of this century. And, while Collier borrowed much in plot, characterization, and tone from the eighteenth century, his novel also resembles Butler's in several important respects, although his hero is vastly different from Butler's gloomy and self-analytic Ernest Pontifex. Pontifex is not a spontaneous and bright-eyed young man buffeted by the winds of change, but a sad boy, fixed permanently in his hopeless course by his heredity.

Collier and the Eighteenth Century. The prose style of *Defy the Foul Fiend* is more elaborately wrought than that of any of his other novels. Sentences are rigorously balanced: "Willoughby was as unaccustomed to wine as he was to love."[1] Lady Stumber, whom Willoughby will eventually try to assault, "was not entirely unconscious of his glance, but neither was she in the least ashamed of her attractiveness; in fact, she held that devotion to her beauties was a sign of virtue second only to devotion to her mind" (31). Occasionally, there is an intentionally obtrusive didacticism, again in the style of the older fiction: "To admire and desire have been condemned as antagonistic to happiness, a censure which is conspicuously undeserved by these emotions in their initial stages" (32). Unlike Collier's other novels, much attention is paid to the manners of the characters, with the eighteenth-century insistence that the quality of a person is judged by the quality of outward behavior, not the sincerity of the intentions or the passions of the soul. Nowhere else does Collier pay so much attention to knives and forks and to gestures with eyeglasses. And he moves his characters to these formal meetings with an atypical reliance upon coincidence, as if London were still the tiny city of an earlier age.

The influence of that age is also manifest in the delineation of certain minor characters. Willoughby Corbo, like his literary ancestors, is a bastard; his father is a decadent rake worthy of the period of the Georges. An alcoholic and a gambler so conscienceless as to rob his own son, the father dies, clearly of venereal disease, in a scene that would be incongruous if it were mingled in any way with nineteenth-century sentimentalism. Such rakes in life existed throughout the Victorian and Edwardian periods, but in the fiction of those periods they were generally toned down. Collier's rakes reflect the more brutal portrayals of the eighteenth century rather than the subdued portraits of his contemporaries.

A similar borrowing is Lady Stumber, who, in her calculating and adulterous way, might well be the Lady Booby of Fielding's *Joseph Andrews*. Her description is much the same; highly mannered, she bears the air of a high-born predator, although Corbo possesses none of the genuine innocence of Joseph Andrews. Corbo would be corrupt, if he only knew how.

In Ollebeare, the family manor in Gloucestershire, and in its resident, the Honourable George Corbo, uncle of the hero, the eighteenth century also is realized. To create that atmosphere, Collier manufactures a ruin, a manor of Cotswold stone last renovated during the reign of the Hanovers. Walking around the house on his first visit, Willoughby sees fallen ceiling and dilapidated blinds. On the library floor, apples lie on newspapers. Apparently sent into barbaric retirement by a young woman whose picture is still treasured, the master of the house is a spiritual descendant of one of Fielding's crude squires. Rough in manners, George Corbo restricts his enthusiasm to the hunting of pheasants, which he shoots with a maniac's gusto.

Collier and Butler.   Both John Collier and Samuel Butler offer autobiographical heroes who share common attitudes toward parents and education. For different reasons, both Corbo and Pontifex are emotionally starved as children, and from their hunger stem many of their later problems. Pontifex is beaten and bullied into submission by his clergyman father and finds some semblance of pleasure only with an aunt and with servants. Corbo is abandoned by his father, shunted aside by an uncle who has unwillingly taken charge of him, and, likewise, seeks comfort with the servants. Corbo's teacher is, in fact, one of the servants. From this man, Corbo learns a romantic view of the traditional rural class structure and a garbled version of sex. Both protagonists, in fact, are kept in ignorance as to the actual workings of their world, and their naiveté concerning sex is the breeding ground for future problems.

Although Pontifex receives a conventional schooling at Roughborough (Butler's own Shrewsbury) and at Cambridge, and Corbo receives none whatsoever except what he can acquire on his own, both heroes are used by their authors to illustrate the ill effects of an impractical education in later life. Pontifex, leaving school, is totally incompetent to hold any position except that of clergyman; he is saved, finally, by inherited wealth from his aunt. Corbo in desperation is sent as secretary to a political figure of limited power and intelligence; he bluffs his way into the job, but it is clear that he has no idea as to even the amenities of an interview. His descent from that tenuous position is rapid, until, finally, he becomes enmeshed in a business venture that makes even Fatigay's scheme for obtaining a fortune through selling matches sound hard-headed and practical. Corbo, too, is finally saved through an inheritance, just as Fatigay, another product of English education, must be raised from the gutter by the efforts of his chimpanzee wife.

Both Pontifex and Corbo turn the relationships between the sexes into nightmares. Like Fatigay, Corbo is healthily sexual; Pontifex is not, approaching his initiation into sex as if he were preparing for an onerous career. Unable to tell a chaste woman from a prostitute, Pontifex rejects the overtures of a prostitute and then, regretting his decision, he attacks a virtuous woman by mistake and is imprisoned. Eventually, in desperation, he marries the former servant who once befriended him, completely blind to her decline into the life of a sloven and an alcoholic. Corbo, with equal innocence, falls romantically in love with the manipulative and adulterous Lady Stumber, who uses his attentions to conceal her affair with another young man. When Corbo's eyes are finally opened, he forcibly attacks her and loses his job as her husband's secretary. Like Pontifex, but with less serious consequences, Corbo also manages to get arrested. Later, again like Pontifex, he mistakes a common whore for a romantic girl until he sees her keeping an appointment with a brute. Just as Pontifex marries the servant, so Corbo, disillusioned, bitterly resolves to marry one of the next whores he encounters, simply on the basis of the woman's obvious ugliness. Corbo finally does marry the heroine of the book; in the Butler novel, there is no heroine. But, by the end of the novels, both men have so mismanaged their lives as to be incapable of any kind of sane relationship with any woman.

Plot

As the story begins, Lord Ollebeare presents the infant Willoughby to his brother Ralph and disappears, trusting that the baby's helplessness will touch the heart of his sister-in-law. It does. Her reward for her good-heartedness, however, is that she dies of a disease she catches while nursing him. Willoughby is deposited in the country where he remains during the years of the First World War, tutored primarily by an "old centaur" of a servant, a man of seventy with a sense of romance and no sense of proportion (15).

After the war, Ralph Corbo, fearing he is dying of cancer, recalls the boy's existence and approaches Lord Ollebeare about finding him a job. Ralph loses interest when he begins to recuperate. Lord Ollebeare, now down on his luck, wields little influence, and so Willoughby takes a job as secretary to the third-rate Lord Stumber. There he falls in love with Lady Stumber, who is having an affair with a young man named Baiye.

Baiye is touched by Willoughby's innocence. He and a group of his friends, a gathering reminiscent of the Finches of the Grove in *Great Expectations,* entertain Willoughby and attempt to enlighten him by showing off for him. They speak of the art of seduction, which they are not always careful to distinguish from rape. Learning too thoroughly, Willoughby dashes back to the Stumber home to attack the mistress of the house and of Baiye. She naturally protects her virtue, and Willoughby loses his job. At that moment in time, Willoughby sees evidence that Baiye has been there, and his eyes are opened. By the end of the evening, he is drunk. He is arrested.

By coincidence, he encounters his father. Lord Ollebeare cheats him of his money but, in compensation, devises a plan by which Willoughby can extort money from the third brother, George Corbo, who resides at Ollebeare. Shortly after, Lord Ollebeare dies of his disease, preferring death to the abstemious life upon which his physician insists. Willoughby leaves for Ollebeare and meets George Corbo, who, after initial resistence to the disruption of his life, entertains him simply among the ruins and teaches him to shoot. They grow fond of one another, but his uncle, tired of the young man's incessant chatter, ships Willoughby back to London.

In London, Willoughby determines to experience life. He meets a young prostitute whose splendid, silent stupidity causes him to believe her to be a woman of profound sympathy and understanding. Despite her references to the madam of the house where she works, Willoughby innocently offers to elope with her and maintains his illusions until he sees her keeping an appointment with a man of evil appearance and great size. Continuing his adventures among the prostitutes and the other denizens of the streets, he happens upon Baiye, who by now is fascinated by the spectacle that Willoughby presents. Baiye, a languid *fin-de-siècle* aesthete, teaches him something about clothing, food, and art, and encourages him to read such works as the *Golden Ass, Candide,* and *The Letters of John Chinaman.* Unfortunately, a passing acquaintance introduces him to Dostoevsky, "on whom poor Willoughby went absolutely mad" (127).

Influenced by the Russian, Willoughby embarks on a course of suffering which he spreads like a miasma around him. Baiye, whose patience has been tried too far, decants him out into the night, where he is accosted by the homely prostitute whom he identifies with Dostoevsky's Sonya. When he proposes marriage to her, she, not unreasonably, concludes he is insane and has him removed from the premises.

He falls next into the hands of would-be revolutionists and is introduced into London's radical circles, where he is "asked if he was studying art . . . if he had yet turned his attention to Social Credit . . . if he had been analyzed; liked . . . the drama, the male form; would he care to take home a manuscript to read, or go to Paris to collect some packets of powder . . ." (134). Just as he had been converted to Dostoevsky's ideas, so now is he converted by the political left. He proclaims his radicalism and sneers at anything that resembles middle-class manners or comfort.

It is at this point that he falls in love with Lucy Langton, daughter of a conservative treasury official who is unimpressed by Willoughby's dinner-table oratory against the middle class and against all respectable methods of earning a living. Through Lucy, Willoughby first experiences tenderness and a stumbling, but authentic, sensuality, but he will not compromise his current set of principles in order to win her. The lovers are separated. Even without her, Willoughby soon sheds his radical pose.

By now he is in financial straits, and, with Fatigay's impracticality, he determines to win his fortune by selling a washing aid on commission. By the time countless doors have been slammed in his face, he has begun to appreciate the realities of the business world, and he sheds much of the optimism with which he had originally approached London, life, love, and political reform. During this period, however, he has made a lasting friend, an old man who makes an insecure living by addressing envelopes and peddling merchandise of various sorts. Willoughby takes the old man home, befriends him, and listens to him talk about Huxley, Spencer, Bradlaugh, Kropotkin, and the other prophets of progress. Belief in the ideal of progress, in fact, is all that keeps the old man alive. As romantic and lacking in either proportion or sensitivity in his despair as in his other phases, Willoughby talks the old man out of his belief and thus is responsible for his friend's suicide.

While they are housed together in a decaying, bug-ridden Pimlico boarding house among the streets that Collier paints in *Gemini,*

Willoughby, through Baiye, is invited to a party given by a lisping young stage designer. There he meets a number of fashionable young Londoners in an atmosphere of perfume, smoke, and African masks; the party is no more flatteringly presented than is Amy's in *His Monkey Wife*. Among the guests is a very beautiful and extremely promiscuous young woman. Eventually, Willoughby is installed in this girl's apartment and maintained at her expense. Forced to witness her unfaithfulness, he finally recoils against the squalor of the arrangement. Leaving, he proclaims himself to be a Tory.

As he is adopting this new creed, Lucy is being radicalized. Living on the Continent, she has learned to accept many of the attitudes that she rejected when Willoughby lectured her in his radical phase. Returning to England, she is reunited with him and, expecting understanding, she confesses to Willoughby her sexual misdemeanors. She is startled when he is horrified. As passionate a conservative as he was a radical, Willoughby now believes in the double standard; he cannot forgive her. She flies back to the Continent, where finally he pursues her, convincing her to quit her studies, marry him, and return with him to Ollebeare, which he now has inherited.

Willoughby settles down to become a conservative landowner, replicating exactly his dead uncle's habits. His scheme of life leaves no room for the adult Lucy; she is left to pace the floor while he devotes himself to the land and his hunting. His attempt to force her into the life of an eighteenth-century squire's wife is, of course, a failure, although she endures a year before she flees. When Willoughby is last seen, he is instructing his servant to lay newspapers on the library floor so that apples may be stored there again. Like Candide, he will tend his garden, although his is not the formal cultivation envisioned by Voltaire.

Principal Characters

Willoughby Corbo.   Corbo is a *tabula rasa*. Little was imprinted during his boyhood exept his mentor's romanticism and lack of proportion; he brings to his adulthood a mind as bright as tinsel and as valueless. He has learned all he knows from books, and he believes that rules of life can be found if only he reads enough, first novelists and then theorists. He never learns that the world is the Bergsonian world of flux that Collier posits in *Paradise Lost* and that the patterns found in books are merely incomplete, simplistic reductions of reality.

At the beginning, Willoughby thrives on fiction, trusting that some novelist will show him "what sort of fine fellow he should be." He reads widely and randomly, and thus he goes astray, for he has no way of knowing that, in real life, Don Juan would be the kind of "soapy" character popularized by Valentino and "Don Quixote a bloody fool": "When he read of Panurge, he longed to be as merry a villain, and never was shown that what is a knave in a book is in reality a *howling cad*" (19). Thrown out into the world, he knows nothing else to do but to keep reading. Preparing for his interview with Lord Stumber, he decides to imitate Gil Blas. Gaining his new position while still in a state of complete ignorance, he "read more and worse novels to get the tone" for his correspondence, and "the tone he got from them would have suited a Cabinet Minister, to say nothing of Lord Stumber, for popular minds think alike." For emergencies, he keeps a novel in his desk, "sometimes opening a drawer to peep at the appropriate page" (34).

His taste is given new dimensions in London. Baiye's friends talk about figures such as Catullus and about the products of the Pandarus Press, and Baiye himself, of course, attempts to expand Willoughby's mind in other directions. When he first approaches Ollebeare, it is in a mood borrowed from the Georgian poets, and, when he sees the girl's picture that his rural uncle treasures, he instantly recalls Robert Browning. Back in London, he is smitten with an attack of George Moore, while the decadence of De Quincey and Dowson dictates his confrontation with the sublimely stupid young whore.

Dostoevsky is the last novelist to affect him strongly. After his Dostoevsky phase, he passes into the world of political and social theory, until finally, as he is being buffeted by the complexities of poverty, he loses all faith in theory and begins to undermine the old man's optimism. In the last half of the novel, there are few specific literary references except for a splendidly comic passage when, as one of his initial tributes to Lucy's loveliness, he offers her up a copy of *Gulliver's Travels*. At the end of the book, he realizes that he shares the jealousy of Othello. It is not that he finds anything to replace fiction. He does not. Rather, he becomes bankrupt. Since literature offers no rules to make sense of life, he substitutes the posturing of a political ideologue. As is evidenced in the creation of God in *Paradise Lost,* Collier finds only pathos in those who attempt to reduce reality to the limits of their own minds and of simple theories.

Lucy Langton. Lucy, like Eve and Emily, is a well-developed and highly individualized character. Like both, she has a mind of her own, and, because she has this strong sense of self, her strength is greater than that of Willoughby. She is, in fact, a powerful character, so much so that, even as a young lady in an age of convention, she accepts the codes of society and the opinions of others only when these do not do violence to her own needs. Honest, direct, sensual, generous, and humane, she demands from Willoughby the treatment that she grants him; ultimately, she leaves him because she realizes he is, through no fault of his own, incapable of responding in like fashion.

As is the case with Collier's other important women characters, she represents a humanizing force that is tolerant of individual differences and impatient with rigid systems and ideologies. Unlike Willoughby, she will not hurt another person for the sake of principle. Early in her relationship with him, they argue about this matter. In the face of Willoughby's tirades against her father and against what her father represents, she replies: "I know, dearest, you are right on principle. I shall never again believe in all that I did before we met. But one cannot hurt a person one loves upon principle. You must see that" (169). That she will not forsake her father to run off with the then-radical Willoughby is the result of her love for both and her refusal to inflict pain on principle, just as these govern her decision to remain with Willoughby during the year of her marriage, a long act of tolerance on her part during which she suspects she is going mad.

She understands better than Willoughby that, just as she has been shaped by her humane and generous education and treatment during her childhood and young adulthood, so he has been fixed in his course by his inexperience of either and his failure to comprehend them. At the end, Willoughby comes to understand his own sense of defeat, his bitterness, and his futility. He takes solace alone from the land, which remains what it is, regardless of man's enthusiasms, passions, and dogmas: "There is something in me . . . that loves a thing most—loves it quietest and best, then—when first I see it broken and dead. It wasn't always so. The place is, and the life is: that's why everything else must be" (295). Lucy must leave because she cannot stand to be one of his broken and dead things.

The Writing

A reconstruction of an eighteenth-century novel virtually demands a panoramic cast of characters. Novels of manners are effective according to the number of contrasts that can be developed among the characters, and the lengthy introspection of any single character usually comes as an intrusion. In *Defy the Foul Fiend,* Collier successfully deals with this matter, introducing a crowd of characters more varied than in any other of his writings. So well are these characters differentiated by speech patterns that the reader is at no time in danger of forgetting who they are.

In some cases, Collier makes use of conventional devices. Lady Stumber, for example, speaks with the clichés and the excited punctuation of romantic novels. "Oh, you poor silly boy," she says to the aroused Willoughby, "What *have* I done, to make you like this? How I wish I could do something for you!" (36). Lord Ollebeare, Willoughby's father, is highly stylized. Advising Willoughby on the occasion of his son's employment with Lord Stumber, the decaying rake remarks: "How to get on with old Stumber. *Bumber* we called him when we were boys: he succeeded while he was still at school. Ha! Ha! Ha! Hoo! Hoo! Hoo!" (56).

Elsewhere, Collier more imaginatively deals with syntax, logic, and dialect. To re-create the rusticity of George Corbo, master of Ollebeare, Collier breaks down conventional syntactic patterns. Willoughby appears at Ollebeare and identifies himself to George Corbo and his servant, Bucknell, both of whom are preoccupied with hunting and hunts such as that at Crufts. Corbo at first refuses to believe Willoughby: "'That's a lie,' said the other very doggedly. 'I met Ollebeare, February four or five years back—when we went to Crufts, Bucknell, and it wasn't on—he said no woman had got her hooks in him'" (71). Bucknell, in turn, speaks in a convincing dialect: "'Say he may eat, sir,' begged the keeper. 'The young gentleman's fair flagging for want of a bite and a sup'" (72). Willoughby's first and most empty-headed prostitute speaks in a series of monosyllables and logical *non sequiturs*. Willoughby, in his *fin-de-siècle* mood, tells her that her name, Louise, is "like a pearl on black velvet." To this she inanely replies by saying, "I like black velvet. . . . It's nice. A girl was given some pearls by a gentleman and they weren't real" (95). To characterize the hedonistic Baiye, Collier alters syntax so that a disproportionate number of clauses begin with "I." To Willoughby, Baiye observes: "You cannot guess . . . what good entertainment I shall find in you. I only wish I were guileless enough to take it up thoroughly, and to make plans for your education. They would never be realised; still I should enjoy the making of them, if I did not know they would never be realised" (122).

Willoughby's language changes as the winds of his passions shift. Early in the novel, he speaks and thinks in a highly pretentious language. The excitability of the young man is reflected in an abundance of questions and exclamations. Waiting too long for his father, Willoughby fantasizes for no reason that the man has died, saying: "He walked in a very strange, uncertain way. . . . Perhaps he was musing over our strange encounter

. . . when he was knocked down. How sad a dead thing he must look, with that nose, and all his twinkle gone!" He imagines a morgue: "I see him on some horrible slab: it is worse than losing the money. Is it possible that I love him?" (60). With Louise, he unintentionally adopts Baiye's languid tones, while, in his dinner-table oratory at the home of Lucy Langton, he imitates the language of radical pamphleteers, speaking of tradesmen as "the most hateful cancer in all modern life" and of clerks as "part of the capitalist machine" (160). At the end, he becomes less articulate, as when, in the lines quoted in an earlier section, he broods on his love for dead things. Finally, he slips into the language of the country, telling Bucknell: ". . . my notion was to get young 'uns. Six-weeks pigs of good breed, d'ye see? That go for under a pound apiece in these days. Breed and sell, I thought, and keep back the likeliest . . ." (283).

Lucy's language grows from the emotional diction of a young girl in love to the balanced tones of a mature adult with a strong sense of self and a need to assert it. Collier manages the shift by sprinkling her early statements with coordinating conjunctions that give the impression of excitability. When she first refuses to elope with Willoughby, she tells him: "You must be patient, my darling. You've grown up wild and free (and it may be best, as you say), but to me it's not only a principle. He's a person, and I know him so well, and it's been so bad for him since mother died, and he's been so wonderful to me, and I'm so extremely fond of him" (164). As Lucy prepares to leave Ollebeare for the last time, the conjunctions have vanished and a new pronoun has appeared: "Look, my dear. . . . It's nothing to do with loving or not loving. I wish to God you'd been bitten by any other fly than this. I shouldn't have minded. But no other would have stung so deep, I suppose, in one of your nature. I must work things out. I can't do it here. If I do, I know what decision I shall come to. I don't want to be made to come to that decision merely because a place makes one want to scream. I must go away for a long time" (293).

The richness of dialogue is matched by the unflawed architecture of the book as a whole. Even the passages needed to elicit the sense of eighteenth-century atmosphere are woven into the text with great tact. Except in the early chapters, most appear at the beginning of chapters and, when Collier has made his point, he allows his rhetoric to become more natural to a modern eye. Literary borrowings and parodies also are woven in with great subtlety.

The result is a book about a young man that, on the one hand, is as clever as much of Fielding and Smollett and, on the other, is as autobiographical as much of the work of Dickens, Butler, Gosse, and Joyce. Never one to relinquish craftsmanship, a sense of comedy, and a love of language and literature for the sake of naked self-revelation, Collier here has made the best of two traditions and produced an autobiographical novel that, certainly, deserves as much attention as has been paid to Gosse's *Father and Son* or Butler's *The Way of All Flesh* but that still, in the best tradition of eighteenth-century decorum, politely veils the self that is speaking. As in *Paradise Lost* and many of his short stories, Collier is more interested in life, including his own life, as fable or allegory or exemplum than as mere incident and eccentricity, so that *Defy the Foul Fiend* tells not only his own story but that of all young men who, poorly educated and naively romantic, are thrust into a world that proves unexpectedly weird. With Dr. Johnson's Imlac, Collier believed the business of the writer was to examine the species, not merely to count the streaks on the petals of individual flowers.

Chapter Six
Short Fiction: The Forms

A John Collier story is recognizable; it is unique. Most of his approximately fifty stories are reprinted continually, and they seem contemporary, even those first published some thirty years ago. Collier is not a realist, but, unlike Lord Dunsany, with whom he has been compared, he does not exploit the supernatural for its own sake, nor, like Saki, is he writing about horror simply to horrify. Instead, he generally is intent on a Bergsonian illumination of the flux, violence, horror, and possibility that underlie everyday life. This sense of a changing and exciting universe, as has been seen, underlies *Paradise Lost;* fear of it sends the hero of *Defy the Foul Fiend* into full retreat. With a policeman's trained eye, Collier sees patterns beneath the patterns that most humans see. To communicate his vision clearly, he must destroy the reader's conventional expectations, and, to do this, he draws together incongruous elements, some of them also found in his longer works.

Part of his effect in the short stories, as in *Paradise Lost, Defy the Foul Fiend,* and *His Monkey Wife,* is born of his sense of a complex relationship among an author, his contemporaries, and the giants of the past. He borrows from literature as if its writers were close friends. Often, his chamber of contemporary horrors is found embedded in a simple structure that we have been taught to identify with the innocence of childhood. While sometimes he draws upon the literary work of his contemporaries, taking the premises of Dreiser and Galsworthy and imposing new horrors of which the original authors never dreamed, more often he draws upon myth, fairy tale, animal fable, or variations upon the Faust legend. Using those forms to stress the incongruities of existence, he attacks our preconceptions about existence, morality, and bourgeois values.

His use of his literary tradition takes more than one form. He is among the most erudite of popular short-story writers, and literary references are used to add wit and color in the same way they are used in *His Monkey Wife* and *Defy the Foul Fiend*. Such a reference may be extremely complex.

One of the most amusing such usages involves Bernard Shaw's *Caesar and Cleopatra*. In the third act of that play, Cleopatra forces her way into Caesar's presence wrapped in a carpet. This entrance is cited in Collier's Hollywood stories "Gavin O'Leary" and "Pictures in the Fire." In the former, the hero is a performing flea; this may, in fact, be the only extant portrait of a homosexual performing flea who attains great fame and purple evening clothes in Hollywood. The heroine of "Pictures in the Fire" is an inane and avaricious starlet named Belinda Windhover. In both stories, the contrast between the actors and the glamorous figure of Cleopatra is itself a source of humor, but Collier goes farther than that. The desire of Gavin to make such an entrance and Belinda's screenwriter to provide one also satirizes the "cute" meetings so popular with Hollywood actors and directors. On still another level, the references serve to satirize a certain kind of Hollywood ignorance or antiintellectualism. In Shaw's play, Cleopatra is not the queen of the Nile. She is a spoiled, vicious child who, in Act 3, Caesar has yet to educate and to tame. Flea and starlet have heard of Cleopatra; clearly they do not know Shaw and there is reason to believe that they do not know much else. At the same time, since both Gavin and Belinda are as spoiled and self-indulgent as Shaw's Cleopatra at this point in the play, there is, indeed, a similarity among the three that Gavin and Belinda do not realize but that is obvious to a modestly educated reader.

The complexity of this reference illustrates the fact that, while Collier may have written for popular magazines and while he may have written in a pure and polished prose that is readily comprehensible, he basically does not condescend to his reader. This is evidenced everywhere in his style, which enhances the eerie effect of the stories by contrasts that attract and startle the eye.

Often, the weirdest of his stories begins with a disarmingly commonplace paragraph, so that the initial meeting with the devil and hell in "Hell Hath No Fury" and "Fallen Star" is in a commonplace reference to a housing shortage, written in the unimpassioned tone of a news report. It takes the reader a moment to grasp the basic incongruity: the scene is hell.

He brings to this kind of writing, also, the sense of style that glitters through *His Monkey Wife* and *Defy the Foul Fiend*. Sometimes, this takes the form of the interjection of extremely formal sentences, of the type that lends an eighteenth-century tone to the latter novel. This is peculiarly effective in "Gavin O'Leary," simply because of the contrast between the true elegance of diction and the false elegance of Gavin. At that point at which Gavin turns homosexual, the author intrudes with his own voice: "The biographer prefers to draw a veil over the next stage of Gavin's career. To know all is to excuse all, but to know less in a case of this sort is to have less to excuse."[1]

This felicity of language shines through "Sleeping Beauty," in which the source of comedy is the contrast between the English elegance of the protagonist, Edward Laxton, and the crudity of the sleeping girl whom he chooses to romanticize. The story begins with a sentence worthy of Jane Austen, in which the formality of Laxton, as well as the intensity of his acquisitive instinct, is immediately established: "Edward Laxton had everything in the world that he wanted except a sweetheart, fiancée, or wife" (311). The formality of the opening line and of the central character is then comically contrasted with the crudity of Heeber's Bluff, Arkansas, with its sideshow, sleeping beauty, rusty wire, and animal skeletons in scenes that, in their depiction of southern American language, evidence the same fine ear as is evident in *Defy the Foul Fiend*.

In other stories, Collier seems to mirror the attitude of the reptile in Osbert Sitwell's "Subtlety of the Serpent," when that reptile lauds the monkey for being unable to veil its actions with fine words. In Collier's stories, as in the fashionable party scenes of *Defy the Foul Fiend* and *His Monkey Wife,* elegant language may conceal the most malevolent of motives and deeds.

In "Another American Tragedy," for example, two professional men conceal their overwhelming avarice beneath well-turned Baconian aphorisms. In that story, a desperate young man asks to have all his teeth pulled. He intends to rid himself of his wealthy uncle and then to masquerade as that uncle long enough to change the uncle's will in his own favor. At first, his dentist is unwilling to pull a set of healthy teeth, but the young man flashes money beneath the dentist's nose, and the professional's mind is changed. He decides that the young man must be mad to request such a service and that "*mental* derangement is caused by *dental* derangement" (188). His teeth pulled, the young man lies in his uncle's sickbed and calls for the lawyer. A physician comes instead, and the young man suddenly finds that he is being eviscerated by the friendly family doctor. That professional, too, has a way with words. As he tosses parts of the young man's anatomy over the furniture, he explains to the nurse that the patient must be insane. Why else would he want to disinherit the friendly family physician in favor of a worthless nephew? "Mental derangement is often caused by abdominal derangement," he explains, as he continues his work on the young man's stomach (193).

Literary Borrowings

In the short stories as in the longer works, then, Collier expresses his sense of literature as artifice, playing freely with literary styles and forms. In some of his most effective stories, he borrows an idea from another work of fiction and transforms it, usually from a serious work into a miniature comic masterpiece with a serious social point.

"Thus I Refute Beelzy." This story is Collier's single deliberate imitation of Saki, specifically of Saki's story "Sredni Vashtar," in which a fragile ten-year-old boy, Conradin, lives with his cousin and guardian, Mrs. De Ropp, who resents her responsibility. She disguises her own hostility by telling herself that she thwarts the boy for his own good. Conradin returns her loathing with good measure. He takes sanctuary in a tool-shed which he peoples with figures of his imagination, a hen, and a ferret. He creates a religion around the latter. Mrs. De Ropp, seeing his pleasure, decides that whatever he is doing in the shed must be bad for him. She raids the sanctuary with her "pestering and domineering and superior wisdom."[2] The ferret answers the child's prayers and kills the woman.

Collier modernizes the story. As skeptical of the family as a social institution as he is of all other institutions and ideologies, he removes the wicked stepmother figure of Mrs. De Ropp in order to show the cant and hypocrisy that underlie the normal, middle-class family. Mr. Carter prides himself in being a permissive parent; he brags that he is a comrade to his son. Under the surface, however, he is the tyrannical head of household that Butler paints in *The Way of All Flesh*. His permissiveness and friendliness last only so long as he gets his own way.

In public, he humiliates his son and forces the boy to talk about his personal life. What he hears throws him into a rage. The son reveals that he has a private playmate named Mr. Beelzy, and he refuses to admit, despite his father's tantrum, that Mr. Beelzy is merely a figment of his imagination. In fact, forced to choose between the illusion of Mr. Beelzy and the reality of the family, the child insists that Mr. Beelzy is real and the family is an illusion, which is, in a sense, quite true, for Mr. Carter's fury reveals the falsity of the family structure on which he prides himself. The father sends the child upstairs to await a beating, despite the child's warning. Just as Saki's story ends with the bloody mouth of a ferret, so does Collier's end in gore. There is a strange sound. What is left is a man's shoe with a foot still in it, lying on the landing, much "like that last morsel of a mouse which sometimes falls unnoticed from the side of the jaws of the cat" (232).

"Over Insurance."   In "Over Insurance," Collier creates domestic carnage from O. Henry's sentimental "Gift of the Magi." In the original story, young Della and James Young find themselves down to their last $1.87 on the day before Christmas. As a token of her love, Della cuts her magnificent hair and sells it in order to buy a platinum chain for her husband's most prized possession, his grandfather's watch, only to find that her husband has sold that watch so that he might buy a set of expensive combs for her treasured hair. O. Henry ends by comparing these young people to the Magi. He envisions marriage as it ought to be.

Collier envisions marriage as it is. His young couple, Alice and Irwin, are like O. Henry's couple in that they begin in rhapsody, as "happy as any young couple in a family-style motion picture" (118). They fondle each other; they dote, and they adore. Each day Irwin hurries home to enjoy her voluptuous body, while she, at table, picks out "some dainty titbit to pop between his eager and rather rubbery lips" (118). One day, a near-miss in traffic brings Irwin to an awareness of his mortality. He determines to insure himself so that his cherished wife will be comfortable after his death. She, in return, insures herself in his favor as proof of her equal love. So much do they prove their love in this fashion that they reduce themselves to poverty.

With poverty, love departs. Alice's body is no longer rounded and firm; Irwin imagines that he might prefer being greeted at the door by one of the steaks that they no longer can afford. Alice looks at Irwin and fantasizes an omelet. To regain their lost luxuries, each decides to poison the other. Both succeed, and they die together on the doorstep.

"Another American Tragedy."   This story, mentioned earlier for the deftness of its style, is, of course, borrowed from Theodore Dreiser's *An American Tragedy*. In Dreiser's 1925 novel, the hero, Clyde Griffiths, is the victim of his own inner weakness and of social forces that act upon him almost without his awareness. Despite his careful planning of the murder of the poor girl whom he has impregnated and whose death will free him to marry into wealth, the actual killing seems almost accidental, representing the unknown forces that actually have controlled his life and his death.

Like Clyde, Collier's protagonist falls victim to powerful forces. Clyde becomes part of a romantic triangle; Collier's hero inadvertently stumbles into one, a particularly sordid one. A voluptuous nurse, clearly the physician's mistress, has been sent to minister to the uncle's masculine needs and, incidentally, to spy upon the household; she alerts the physician when the young man, posing as his uncle, attempts to change the will. A heavy-set and heavily made-up woman in her thirties, the nurse clearly intends to provide for her future before her failing charms disappear altogether. Collier's hero is governed by greed, but his vice is that of an amateur. His threat to disinherit the physician places him in the hands of members of the professional classes, whose greed dwarfs his own in its intensity and its imaginativeness. Thus, the nephew finds himself being disemboweled.

"Without Benefit of Galsworthy." "Without Benefit of Galsworthy" also presents a romantic triangle. In the title, Collier substitutes the name of a writer he believed to be a sentimentalist in a phrase that more normally reads "without benefit of clergy." The phrase itself was once used in criminal cases where a knowledge of reading—the knowledge of clergy or clericals—might suffice to save a criminal from punishment; it also is the title of a story by Rudyard Kipling. Collier's immediate source was Galsworthy's three-act comedy, *A Family Man.*

In John Galsworthy's play, the protagonist is John Builder, who prides himself on being a model husband, father, and Englishman. In reality, he is a bully. One daughter runs away to live with a man whom she refuses to marry. A second daughter threatens to run away to go into the movies. His wife catches him in the arms of Camille, the French maid, and she, too, makes her escape. All this he blames on modern and radical influences, taking no responsibility himself. The father is so enraged by the women's escapes that, although he himself is a magistrate, he ends by appearing in court, charged with assault. He loses face in the community, a matter of great consequence to him. This court appearance turns the course of the play's action and permits Galsworthy to arrange a happy ending. Although there is no perceptible change in the bully's character, his daughters and his wife pity him. The daughter who is living in sin decides, after all, to marry her friend. The other daughter inexplicably abandons her dreams of a career. The French maid vanishes, and the wife returns home, presumably to continue her career as her husband's victim.

Without benefit of Galsworthy's sentimentality, Collier seems to be saying, this story would not have a happy ending. Collier's protagonist is not a magistrate but a retired major, a *pukka sahib.* Like Builder, he imagines himself to be a man of great charm, and he blames the misfortunes of his life and marriage on "sneaking Socialists," "bloody Bolsheviks," "blasted agitators," "reptiles from Moscow," and "cursed Reds" (154, 155, 156, 157, 158). The story is told by the major, whose first-person narration turns into an exercise in self-revelation worthy of a Robert Browning monologue.

The major's primary problem is his wife, who is, he says, sound, but who undeniably is aging. He regards her much as he would his horse or dog, but he lusts after his maid, a girl named Gladys. After seeing Gladys naked on the beach, he decides his wife does not understand him. To win Gladys, he determines to sacrifice his standing in the community, a matter of great importance to him, and to break his wife's heart. He accomplishes only the former. His wife is only too happy to leave, staying only long enough to make sure she receives an adequate settlement; whatever happens to the major, there is no chance that she will return to serve as his doormat. She goes, and the major prepares to tell Gladys of her good fortune; an even more solid English husband than Galsworthy's, he has not approached her while his wife was in the house. In Galsworthy's play, the maid is willing to dally with the master, but she is not willing to take the place of the downtrodden wife who leaves. In Collier's more realistic version, the maid will not even begin to dally with a bully. She, too, flies, and the major, like Builder, continues to blame his misfortune on extraneous and irrelevant political forces.

"A Matter of Taste."   This story is based on a device used by many writers of detective fiction; a group of guests, generally friends, sits around at a party or a meeting, and, in the course of their discussions, a crime is solved. The seed of this kind of story may well lie in Robert Louis Stevenson's "The Suicide Club," a story in his 1882 *New Arabian Nights*. Nicholas Blake (C. Day Lewis) used this structure in "The Assassin's Club," which appeared in *Murder for the Millions* along with Collier's own "Back for Christmas," and Ben Hecht used the device in "The Fifteen Murderers." It is still used by Isaac Asimov in his Black Widowers tales. It is difficult to determine any precise source for Collier's story, but he was probably influenced by Agatha Christie's 1933 *Tuesday Club* tales. The central figure in these stories is the gentle nonentity Miss Jane Marple.

Collier's gathering takes place at the Medusa Club. Present are several characters reminiscent of Christie's. One is an Egyptologist whose specialty is asps. Another is a psychiatrist who specializes in homicidal impulses, and there is "an amiable nonentity whose simple utterances are not always unworthy of attention."[3] The gathering also includes a consulting pathologist at the Home Office whose name, Sir Barnard Wigmore, vaguely suggests the famed pathologist Sir Bernard Spilsbury, although Miss Christie uses an ex-commissioner of Scotland Yard. Collier's nonentity could well be her Miss Marple.

What Collier does with this gathering is create pure literary spoof without satire other than of the detective-story form. His characters discuss highly improbable means of murder of the type invented by detective writers in what is now termed the Golden Age of that form. An explorer talks about melting daggers made of ice that leave no evidence, while the psychiatrist offers a mode of inducing suicidal mania.

The actual crime involves a box of poisoned chocolates. Since the eater of the chocolates died, it has been inferred that the chocolates were poisoned, but Sir Barnard Wigmore can find no trace of any toxic substance. At last, the murder weapon is discovered. The killer, a chemist of great talent, has created a flavor so appetizing that the victim has eaten herself to death. Wigmore and the Commissioner of Scotland Yard together swallow, compulsively, the candies that the victim did not get around to eating.

Fairy Tales and Myth

Fairy tales, in Bruno Bettelheim's words, "state an existential dilemma briefly and pointedly."[4] Collier would not quarrel with the assumption of Freud and Bettelheim that the universal experiences of man are presented in these forms. He would quarrel with the notion that children outgrow the situations. Using titles and characters from fairy tales and myths, Collier shows that humans remain helplessly locked in the childish problems, in large part because the adult never outgrows the child's need to find or to create order in the world or the child's desire to return to the unflawed pleasures of Eden.

"Sleeping Beauty." Collier's retelling of this story in the 1930s gave it a feminist cast long before such interpretations became popular. His version emphasizes elements currently discussed by feminist critics; in presenting the story in this way, he is consistent with his recasting of Eve in *Paradise Lost* and with his portrait of the self-actualizing Emily in *His Monkey Wife*.

In Andrew Lang's edition of the original tale, seven fairies are invited to the christening of a princess.[5] An eighth, uninvited, feels slighted, and her gift is that the child should be pricked by a spindle and die of the wound. Another fairy transforms that death into a century-long sleep at the end of which the princess will be awakened from her sleep by the appearance of a prince. In the traditional psychoanalysis of this tale, the long sleep represents the lengthy and silent "concentration" that an adolescent girl needs as she passes through puberty to sexual awakening. More recently, feminist critics have observed that in this story, as in "Cinderella," the moral is that passivity and beauty alone are valued in the female and that rewards will come without effort, as if by magic, to women who possess these qualities. In poet Louise Bernikow's words, men serve as "hypodermic needles," injecting all the life the woman requires.[6] Men, she adds, value these myths because they satisfy male needs: "If you 'get' a woman for your wife who is virgin and enforce chastity in your married life, you, the patriarch, might have a chance at keeping social order, developing laws of inheritance and imagining that you have got some aspect of human life and history under control."[7] To some extent, this patriarchal figure represents Collier's portrait of Adam in *Paradise Lost;* it entirely describes the hero of Collier's "Sleeping Beauty."

Edward Laxton aspires to perfection. As his story begins with the well-rounded opening sentence cited earlier, he possesses an elegant Regency house set in a park; apart from the absence of an Eve from his Eden, his life is one of flawless tidiness. His searches for Eve have so far met with failure, for the women he has met are imperfect. Some wear too much makeup. Others have thick ankles.

A friend invites him to the United States. Driving back across the country to the East Coast, he has an accident in Heeber's Bluff, Arkansas, a dreadful little town filled with people whose primary occupation is the extortion of money from travelers like Laxton. Stranded and wretched, he visits a carnival, and there he sees a sleeping beauty. Without regard for the nature of the woman or for the quality of the people he finds himself among, he decides she is the perfection he has been seeking. Since this is the twentieth century, her sleep is caused by a hormonal imbalance, not a magic spell, and he decides he can cure her.

In the original story, the beauty is awakened with a kiss, but this, again, is the twentieth century, and Collier pokes fun once more at contemporary commercialism. This Prince Charming must purchase his princess. What is more, he is forced to pay for her several times over, since he is blackmailed twice before he can remove the girl to England. Once, he is accused of violating the Mann Act, a problem not contemplated in the stories of Grimm or Perrault. At considerable cost, he takes her to England, but now he can afford only a cottage on the estate he once owned.

Now, he consults a modern sorcerer, an endocrinologist. The medicine man succeeds in breaking the spell. The girl awakens and speaks her first words, some of them profane and others merely tasteless. In an appalling accent, she identifies herself as Susie-May and complains that he has ruined her career in show business. The product of the age of Freud, Laxton is still convinced that the problem has a cure, just as, in *Paradise Lost,* Adam is sure that Eve can be controlled. What he is hearing, Laxton decides, is merely the result of childhood scars; spiritual beauty must surely exist where there is such physical perfection. He exposes her to the beauty of nature, assuming that her personality will be transformed. It is not, but she does succeed in meeting the new owner of the estate, a fleshly man who offers her a career in films.

Obviously, what Laxton craves is a sleeping beauty, not a waking one. He is happy only when he takes her pills away and she returns to her coma.

When last seen, he is recovering his fortune by exhibiting the sleeping beauty in a carnival.

   "Bottle Party." Much the same picture of relations between women and men is painted in "Bottle Party," Collier's retelling of a story that appears as "The Fisherman and the Jinny" in the *Arabian Nights* and as the "Spirit in the Bottle" in *Grimm's Fairy Tales.* The Grimm story relates the tale of a poor student; in the *Arabian Nights,* he is a fisherman. Of course, in the twentieth century, he must, in Collier's opinion, be something more commercial, so the hero is transformed into Franklin Fletcher, a shopper in the vast bazaar that is New York. In the *Grimm* version, the student seeks money, while, in the *Arabian Nights,* he only wishes to rid himself of an evil genie. Not so Collier's hero, who has seen too many films and who, clearly, has seen or read Elinor Glyn's *Three Weeks,* for he is obsessed with the vision of a beautiful woman on a tiger skin. At the age of thirty-five, he not unnaturally has found neither skin nor woman.

   Like Laxton, he wants perfection. In a little shop, he buys a bottle that contains a genie. The genie is cooperative. At Fletcher's request, the genie brings him the most beautiful and seductive women of history— Cleopatra, Guinevere, Helen of Troy, Madame de Pompadour, Lady Hamilton. As it turns out, these women and their tiger skins are not enough. Fletcher wants his seductresses to be virgins. He, too, subscribes to the belief that perfect women are passive and untouched, awaiting a man to give them life. He demands that he be that man. Unfortunately, the great vamps of history are not likely to be passive or chaste, and Fletcher's demand is clearly ludicrous. What he needs is not a woman but a spirit, and so the genie returns to the shop.

   This time, the genie brings Fletcher a bottle containing a beautiful female genie. Fletcher releases her, and she seems perfect. Still, he is suspicious. Thinking that she might have hidden a lover in the bottle, he enters the bottle himself to investigate. There he is imprisoned, as the two spirits, finally united, cavort and frolic. In a sense, seeking perfection, he has created for himself the same kind of bell jar that Collier's God creates in *Paradise Lost;* to desire an end to time and change is to build oneself a prison. Fletcher's bottle is returned to the shop, where, years later, the proprietor sells it, still believing that it contains a beautiful woman. The purchasers are sailors and are as greedy as Fletcher. When they discover that they have bought Fletcher, "their disappointment knew no bounds, and they used him with the utmost barbarity" (8).

   "The Frog Prince." This work is Collier's retelling of the story that appears in the Grimm collection as "The Frog-King, or Iron Henry." In Grimm's story, a princess plays by a well and accidentally tosses her favorite toy, a golden ball, into the water. It is retrieved by a frog who asks that, as a reward, he be allowed to serve as her companion. He keeps his part of the bargain, but the child runs home and forgets her promise until the frog appears at her door to remind her. Her father insists that she keep her word, and she does so despite her revulsion. The frog ends in her bedchamber where, in disgust, she throws him against a wall. As he lands, he becomes a handsome prince.

Bettelheim interprets the story as a parable of the process of maturation; the child tries to resist responsibility but the superego, personified by the king, insists and prevails, and the result is the felicity of sexual awakening. The frog is a frog, Bettelheim contends, because a child's initial reaction to sex is a recognition of its ugliness.[8]

Certainly, Collier's protagonist, Paul, in "The Frog Prince" witnesses a transformation and confronts the possible ugliness of sex. A rich man has a sister. She is twenty-eight years old, stands considerably more than six feet high, and is proportioned appropriately. She is also mentally retarded, although she is able to write adoring fan letters to prize fighters. The rich man suggests to Paul, who is poor, that Paul might marry this woman. Paul agrees and informs his mistress, Olga, of his intention. She receives the news with suspicious restraint, and she vanishes, but, when Paul goes to Boston to woo the rich woman, he finds that she is already married to a Mr. Colefax, who is Olga disguised in male dress. The situation suggests the plight of Sir Leslie Barker, the husband who turned out to be a woman and whose story, cited earlier, is recounted in *Just the Other Day.*

To her own surprise, Olga becomes fond of her innocent bride, sensing an interesting personality beneath the unprepossessing exterior; it is significant that Collier permits a female character this degree of sensitivity, which is denied to male characters like Edward Laxton and Franklin Fletcher. As does Laxton, Olga seeks out a medical man to put the situation right. After treatment, the wife is revealed to be a handsome and adequately intelligent young man. Olga reveals herself to be a woman, and they fall in love. Olga writes to dismiss Paul; she has promised her newly discovered husband never to deceive him again.

The parallels here with the original story and with Bettelheim's interpretation are marked. A childish young sophisticate, comparable to Amy in *His Monkey Wife,* learns responsibility while merely seeking wealth. In the process of growing up, she works through sexual revulsion to sexual awakening, and the ending is happy as in the fairy tale. Paul, who remains fixed in his childish greed, is left on the sidelines to watch with envy.

"**Spring Fever.**" Collier turns from fairy tale to myth in "Spring Fever," this time adapting the story of Pygmalion and Galatea. In the original story, which appears in Ovid's *Metamorphoses,* Pygmalion, a sculptor thoroughly disgusted with women, resolves never to marry. He falls in love with a statue, and Aphrodite, answering his prayers, brings the statue to life. They fall in love. In keeping with his general tendency, Collier transforms this story to emphasize the vulgarity and commercialism of the twentieth century.

In Collier's story, the sculptor hero, Eustace, is a realistic artist, and the twentieth century has no place for his kind of art. Impoverished, he resolves to abandon his ideals and to imitate the art of Edgar Bergen and Charlie McCarthy. He envies Bergen's income. He studies ventriloquism, digs clay from his yard, and vows to create a figure appropriate to the contemporary world. He does so, making a splendid male dummy with the vulgar good looks of an early-day film star.

No goddess wakes this dummy. Instead, he is roused by the physical presence of Eustace's coarse girl friend, Sadie. In fact, his first human gesture is to pinch her. Eustace goes on stage with the dummy and proves so much of a failure that he is hissed off stage. Naturally, Sadie turns on him, and she and the dummy heap scorn on him for his ineptitude. This wakened statue is indeed modern. He has a modern set of values; he wants money. The dummy takes Sadie on his knee and insists that Eustace play the dummy in all future performances. Disillusioned and deserted by Sadie and the dummy, Eustace retires to manufacture tombstones, and, although he has an idea for a quite delightful statue of Eve, he thinks better of the whole notion and transforms the statue into the image of a Sealyham terrier.

"**The Devil George and Rosie.**" Occasionally, Collier will create a tale in which only enough of a mythic reference is present to create the tone of a legend. This is the case with "The Devil George and Rosie," in which the voluptuous female character is at least superficially related to Persephone, the daughter of Zeus and Demeter. Persephone, of course, represents the earth's fecundity. After she is kidnapped by Pluto, she is sought by her mother until finally Persephone is permitted to return to earth for six months of each year. Rosie, too, represents life-giving forces. She is shipped to hell by accident. She is not dead, and her vitality overwhelms all the forces that hell can pit against her.

Actually, the greatest portion of the story is given over to the depiction of a hell that in many ways resembles that of Shaw's *Man and Superman.* It is a hell of pleasure. When the hero, George, arrives to serve as the devil's overseer, a position for which he is eligible by reason of his misogyny, he finds poker games, fireworks, and dirty pictures. When the devil wants to torment his victims, the worst he can do is to dress them in rags and suggest that their neighbors are wearing fine clothes or to isolate them in sordid homes and suggest that their neighbors are enjoying themselves at parties. For Collier, as for Shaw, a permanence of preoccupation with modern pleasures is more miserable a fate than the torments by fire envisioned in earlier ages.

Rosie, naturally, is not part of the parade of shrews, adulteresses, emancipated women, slovens, gossips, teases, and women novelists who have so poured into hell in recent times as to present the devil with a housing problem. Rosie simply is, and her growing love for George, which results in her willingness for him to seduce and corrupt her, baffles the essential conventionality of the devil and the bureaucratic red tape of hell. There is no other solution but for George to flee with her back to earth, where time and change and the potential of tragedy are infinitely more desirable than any permanence the devil can offer.

Animal Fables and Stories

Collier created several kinds of animal stories. Often, the use of animals creates a fablelike tone. As in *His Monkey Wife,* animal behavior may be used as a standard against which human behavior is measured and found wanting. In such stories as "Gavin O'Leary," weird human behavior is placed in a moral context by being ascribed to an animal or insect; in the spirit of a Chaucer or Spenser, the person who evidences this behavior is something less than or other than human. Two published stories are simply animal stories, direct and straightforward. "Mademoiselle Kiki" and "Son of Kiki" are stories of a waterfront cat in La Caillot, a village near Marseilles. These stories are charming, but, because they lack the comic incongruities of the other tales, they are far less effective and memorable.

"Variation on a Theme."   The tone of this early story reflects that of *Just the Other Day,* where Collier and Lang express disgust at the shallowness and vulgarity of much fashionable literature. Here, too, is reflected a total distaste for the manipulations of the literary marketplace with its cocktail parties and its panderings to the artificial and arbitrary taste of reviewers who pass judgment on the basis of personal whim rather than of considered standards, taste, and judgment.

The basic conflict in this story is between man and ape, and neither is particularly human. Both are, or pretend to be, novelists. Grantly, the human writer, prides himself on the great delicacy and taste of his life and art; he is a stylist. He yearns, however, to have one of his books selected by the Book Society. He speaks in long, rather latinate sentences, heavily punctuated by exclamation points and by critical jargon, and he is married to an artistically pretentious woman who speaks in banalities. The gorilla, on the other hand, is modern man. His modernism may well be indicated by the fact that he bears the name of Ernest Simpson, the mild-mannered and complaisant husband of the future Duchess of Windsor; the scandal involving Mrs. Simpson and the heir to the throne was well known, if little publicized, at the time this story was written. At any rate, the gorilla has renounced style. His art, as Grantly describes it, is the art of "the grunts, groans, and screams of women with great primeval paps . . ." (292). He speaks and thinks more or less in the style of Hemingway.

Both gorilla and man complete novels. Grantly is concerned that the style of his own social satire is dated and that literature is moving toward the primitive—"fecund women, the urge of lust, blood hatred, all that, you know" (294). He is assured that the reigning reviewer is about to be married to a rather vital young woman and will very soon have had quite enough of the primitive. It is anticipated that, shortly after the wedding, the critic will return to his earlier interest in pure style.

Learning of this, the gorilla switches manuscripts in order to claim Grantly's as his own. But the ape errs. He seizes the critic's fiancée at a party, an amatory effort that earlier had proven successful with Grantly's wife. The critic is enraged, and when Grantly's manuscript is published under Simpson's name, the critic dismisses it in two words, whatever his private opinion of its literary merit. What is more, the gorilla is attacked by some blackshirts who take offense at Grantly's political satire, and he is arrested and tried for "blasphemy, ordinary libel, obscene libel, criminal libel, sedition, and other things . . ." (297). Grantly, it would seem, had been more effective than usual. Simpson's own work, printed under Grantly's name, is, of course, a critical success. Grantly ends with wealth and fashionable approval, while Simpson ends once more looking out from behind bars, this time not the bars of a zoo but those of a prison.

"**Gavin O'Leary.**" Collier's amused contempt for the world of fashionable literature and entertainment takes a new form in "Gavin O'Leary," the previously mentioned story of a performing flea. To the attitudes expressed in "Variation on a Theme," Collier adds the reflections of his Hollywood years.

O'Leary, a born actor, assumes the character of the person whose blood he sucks, whoever that may be. Since his first host is an innocent Vermont girl named Rosie O'Leary, he begins as a happy and healthy, if not wise, individual. But Rosie loses him in a movie house. She is a fan, and her shivering delight so fills her circulatory system that, drinking her blood, Gavin drowsily succumbs to what seems like a fit of drunkenness. Recovering, he next attaches himself to a young man who adores the film star Blynda Blythe. Naturally, Gavin falls in love with her himself and pursues her to Hollywood.

By a combination of bumptiousness and skill, he forces his way into the film business and soon becomes a featured player opposite Blynda, who, unfortunately, is in love with a handsome and shallow actor. Of course, Gavin drinks in this love with Blynda's blood. Adoring the actor, he next becomes a homosexual, since the actor loves no one but himself. In his new guise, Gavin becomes a Hollywood scandal. People gossip about "his fantastic costumes, his violet evening suits, his epicene underwear, his scent-spray shower-bath, and of strange parties at his bijou house in Bel Air" (215). He is graylisted as a menace to the principles of democracy, and there is a threat that his films will be boycotted by guardians of American morality.

But the actor's career fails. In a stroke of cunning and desperation, Gavin arranges that his Vermont hostess, Rosie, be brought to Hollywood. She becomes an actress, and, of course, with her career come shallowness and narcissism. Since Gavin reattaches himself to her and since, now, both of them passionately love her, it is inevitable that they will live happily forever after.

"**Mary.**"   The narcissism of the performing artist is also a theme in this story, which is about a pig named Mary. She belongs to an exceptionally naive young rustic who hopes to make his fortune with her. Curried, pampered, and deified, Mary has developed the raging ego of the star. When the master marries a young woman, again named Rosie, Mary focuses her efforts on arranging matters so that husband and wife have no privacy and the attention of both is concentrated on her own creature comforts.

Sex does not enter the picture for, like so many of Collier's young men, this man knows nothing about it. While Fatigay and Willoughby at least know that sex exists, Mary's master has not arrived even at that level of sophistication. As is the case of Collier's other characters who bear the name Rosie, the bride is vital and forceful, but she is also innocent, and it takes her some time to realize that she must dispose of Mary if ever she is to get her husband alone and teach him those things he should know. In the context of the story, the disposal of Mary is remarkably like the perpetrating of a murder; it is accomplished by a rational appeal to Mary's greed and vanity that allows Rosie to lure Mary away to be ground into sausage. The next morning, the couple blissfully indulges in a superior grade of sausage that neither has ever enjoyed before, and it is obvious that the husband has been a willing and enthusiastic student of his wife.

Faust Stories

Figures from hell appear in many of Collier's writings, often to point to the unimaginably rich possibilities of the universe. In *Paradise Lost,* of course, Satan is a creative force, while in "The Devil George and Rosie" he is merely an unexpected tempter trying to lure humans from the richness of life to an eternity of tawdry pleasures. Often, Collier uses variations on the Faust tale; there are so many such stories that they deserve a separate category of their own. Usually, these figures serve to act out parts much like those in "The Devil George and Rosie."

"Halfway to Hell." Louis Thurlow, hero of "Halfway to Hell," is an elegant young dandy, brought to the brink of suicide by a shallow girl much like Amy in *His Monkey Wife.* Even as he approaches death, Louis remains a poseur, tastefully arranging his features with a view to being found the next morning. Taking his drug, he himself makes a discovery. There is life after death, and a suicide unwittingly contracts for an eternity of a life that contains the most sordid aspects of life on earth. Thurlow's first cue is the appearance of a devil who has caught a headcold waiting for him.

As if the prospect of an eternity of headcolds were not enough, Thurlow next discovers that the entrance to hell is beneath a subway station at Piccadilly Circus, with all the cramming together of unwashed humanity that this implies. Below the more orthodox subway entrance is another, lined with pictures advertising the more fashionable vices. Thurlow is alarmed, and, since humans when desperate are cleverer than those demons engaged in fashionable vices, he manages to get the devil drunk, substituting his rival for the lady's affection for himself. He wakes again at his hotel, thinks seriously about calling the lady, and leaves for France instead.

"The Right Side." In this similar story, the would-be suicide is wandering languorously on Westminster Bridge. His name is Philip Westwick, and he also has been scorned by a lady. As he sadly is about to leap from the bridge, he is accosted by an older man dressed somewhat in the style of G. K. Chesterton. This, too, is a devil.

This time, the hero is escorted to a Fun Fair off Tottenham Court Road and is threatened with an eternity of popular entertainment in a scene evocative of Shaw's "Don Juan in Hell." First he sees grubby men peering through stereoscopes at even grubbier scenes of Parisian nightlife, while others gamble and still others proposition women. Taken further into hell, Westwick confronts a giant movie theater and a dance lounge. Hell, it seems, is people enjoying themselves in the manner of the 1920s and 1930s, a point similar to that which Collier made in *His Monkey Wife* and *Defy the Foul Fiend* with his portraits of lifeless lechery. Westwick meets Ophelia, who, as another suicide, is condemned to an eternity in a dance hall.

Westwick is offered fifty years of Helen of Troy in return for his soul, but he has had enough. He, too, evades the contract. He finds himself back on the bridge, this time to jump down on the right side, the pavement side.

"Pictures in the Fire."   Like "Gavin O'Leary," "Pictures in the Fire" shows the influence of Collier's Hollywood experience. The hero is a writer who will do anything for money, including sell his soul to the devil, which he does. The devil is a newcomer to Hollywood, where he aspires to become a film tycoon, a task for which his talents are eminently suited. He finds himself outclassed, however, for he becomes involved with the ravenous ego of an ambitious actress, Linda Windflower, whose language is that of *Photoplay* and whose aspirations are those of a hungry tiger. No sooner does the devil meet one of her requests than she makes another, each more outrageously expensive than the last. She justifies all by referring to the sacredness of her art. Finally, she bankrupts the devil, who by now is so flustered that he forgets to pick up the option on the contract he holds with the writer, who returns to Malibu.

"Fallen Star."   This time, the Faustian contract is between a minor fiend, Tom Truncheontail, and a fallen angel. Truncheontail flees the radio and television that provide entertainment in hell and, considered in hell as a chronic unemployable and a burden on the community, he takes up residence as a beachcomber on the edge of hell. From this vantage point, he sees the beauty of a she-angel who has fled the summer resorts of heaven to take a swim merely for the sake of breaking rules.

In order to corrupt the she-angel and to get her totally in his power, Truncheontail tosses her to earth to be seduced. She appears as a falling star over Brooklyn Bridge and is later found running naked in Central Park. This naturally leads to a hospital where she falls into the hands of a psychoanalyst. The doctor is a man of high principles, but, like all Collier's professionals, his principles prove flexible when he is faced with temptation. He decides that intimacy with the girl will cure her of her amnesia.

Eventually, they marry, but seven years later the devil returns to claim her. The girl confesses her identity to her husband, who confronts the devil, "for these old, gross, and sensual devils are like scared and sullen children when a psychoanalyst gets hold of them" (53).

The devil is helpless against the narrowness and rigidity of the psychiatrically trained mind. Educated to translate whatever occurs in the universe into the jargon of psychoanalysis, the doctor responds to the devil with a variation on the concept of penis envy and treats him as a classically trained analyst might treat a woman: the demon has a tail, and basic to the demon's dissatisfaction is his envy of those humans who have no tails. But, the analyst claims, the tail is "purely psychic in origin" (53). Producing his best couchside manner, the analyst shortly convinces the fiend that his problems are a function of profound maladjustment which in turn is caused by being born a devil. Before long, the fiend is pleading to be analyzed. So well is he cured that he becomes a success on Wall Street and thus is able to endow a clinic for the analyst.

Chapter Seven
Short Fiction: The Themes

The world of Collier's imagination is a Bergsonian world, rich in texture, color, and Rabelaisian possibilities. There is in it a force, a vitality, that, as in *Paradise Lost,* manifests itself in the form of magic or creativity. That power, however, is not always benign. Evil exists and appears with the unexpectedness of a traffic accident. Regardless of all this, Collier's world is glorious, and part of its beauty is its complexity that defies systematic explanation. Those who attempt to force order on this universe are ridiculous, and in their silliness Collier finds many of his themes.

A few of the stories simply illustrate the existence of magic. Such a story is "Green Thoughts," one of the earliest of his short works. Here evil is incarnate in human form, which is to be expected. But it appears also in a vegetable, a simple product of Mother Nature, and that effect is quite startling. The story is simple. A man inherits a plant. His name is Mr. Mannering, and he possesses the elegance of an Edward Laxton with all of Laxton's desire for order and perfection and with all of his moral myopia. Watching without emotion as his cat and his Cousin Jane are devoured by the plant, appearing recognizably as buds on its sides, Mr. Mannering suddenly finds himself its next victim. He learns wisdom only as he waits helplessly, knowing that he will be killed by his greedy nephew, who will inherit under his will and who has no more moral sensitivity than had, formerly, his uncle. Most of Collier's fiction, however, takes the form of warm-blooded and enthusiastic assaults on those humans and institutions that seek to reduce the universe to a simple set of rules, laws, conventions, or statistics.

One such institution is marriage. For Collier, honor, faith, and integrity between men and women are vital, but none of these qualities has much to do with ordinary marriages, which are governed primarily by convention and acquisitiveness. Ordinarily, the institution pushes those involved to the point of adultery, if not of homicide. Moreover, the institution pits each tiny family tribe against the community at large, so that the tribe operates according to a principle of self-interest that violates the generosity and tolerance that alone make civilized life possible. Many of Collier's goriest stories are domestic ones.

A few of his domestic dramas are presented in the form of myths, some cited earlier. That form, of course, emphasizes the universality of the story being told, and somewhat the same effect is achieved by borrowings from other authors. Such stories include "Mary," "Over Insurance," "Without Benefit of Galsworthy," "Sleeping Beauty," "Three Bears Cottage," "Bird of Prey," and "After the Ball."

Other domestic dramas are presented in more realistic terms, although, however straightforward the style, the events described still bear Collier's unique and macabre touch. This second group of stories includes "De Mortuis," "Wet Saturday," "Little Memento," "Midnight Blue," "Back for Christmas," "Rope Enough," "The Chaser," and "Ah, the University."

The protagonists of these stories often are professional men, for closely related to Collier's attitude toward the bourgeois institution of marriage is his stance toward the bourgeois mind. As bungling or murderous heroes, lawyers, scientists, tradesmen, and industrialists appear in a singular number of stories. He does not write about the working-class man except to pity him and to deplore his entertainments, nor is he, in his stories, interested in the man of independent wealth. In his handling of professional persons, Collier harks back to the point of view presented by young Willoughby Corbo in *Defy the Foul Fiend,* when Corbo lectures Lucy's father on the impossibility of making an honest income in a capitalistic society.

The legal and scientific mind is most likely to be simplistic in its approach to its world. That kind of mind is also easily threatened and shattered when its laws and principles prove incongruous with the world around it. Moreover, in attempting to reduce the world to rigid rule, this type of mind represses emotion. That unrecognized emotion seethes, with great volatility, only to explode as in "The Touch of Nutmeg Makes It," or it emerges in weird rationalization as in "Another American Tragedy" or "Fallen Star." Variations on these themes appear in "Back for Christmas," "Great Possibilities," "Youth from Vienna," and "Interpretation of a Dream," among other stories.

Tradesmen, industrialists, and other commercial men tend, in Collier's stories, to be persons of hardened sensibilities. They are less avaricious than professional men, but, perhaps, only because they tend to have fewer opportunities for unleashed self-indulgence. And they do contaminate what they touch with their commercial values. As what Willoughby

Corbo would call lackeys of society, rather than its masters, they are also exceptionally sensitive to the opinions of others and, being relatively powerless as corporate figures, they also seem to take undue pleasure in showing off what power they have. Such figures include the American businessman Thomas P. Rymer in "The Invisible Dove Dancer of Strath-pheen Island," who, in his dealings with something mysterious and fragile, reveals the soul of a rapist and murderer. They also include the industrialist of "The Steel Cat," who behaves with pure sadism in his dealings with weaker and more vulnerable creatures, man and mouse alike. The mind of the commercial classes, or the result of the prevalence of that mind in society, is again revealed in "Evening Primrose," "Midnight Blue," "Witch's Money," and "Romance Lingers, Adventure Lives," although the small businessmen of the latter are rather more the miserable victims of the system than its villains.

Collier also ridicules the commercial entertainers and artists who pander to the vanity of this society. The most ridiculous of creatures, of course, are the Hollywood stars such as the actress in "Pictures in the Fire" and the flea in "Gavin O'Leary." Not only do they accept the middle-class habit of simplifying the world, but they attempt to reduce that world to the dimensions of their own egos. Much the same kind of figure is presented in "Cancel All I Said," in which the voice of the Hollywood mystique intervenes to destroy a middle-class, supposedly intellectual, family.

Other poets and entertainers, if they are concerned with public opinion, are also satirized, as are the man and the gorilla in "Variation on a Theme" and the writer who sells his soul in "Pictures in the Fire." In the cases of the few real artists who appear and who tend to subvert the system, there is gentle and sympathetic treatment. This is the case in "The Possession of Angela Bradshaw" and "Night! Youth! Paris! and the Moon!" Or such an artist may be totally thwarted, as is Eustace, who makes the ventriloquist's dummy in "Spring Fever."

Domestic Dramas

"Back for Christmas." In 1910, American-born "Dr." Hawley Harvey Crippen poisoned his wife and ineffectively attempted to carve up her body, burn her bones, and bury the remains in his cellar. It was generally admitted that he was not without his reasons. Apparently a mild-mannered man, he was married to a dominating personality who thoroughly henpecked and cowed him. But after his wife's death, Crippen stupidly aroused gossip by bringing his secretary, Ethel Le Neve, to his home and by giving her some of his wife's possessions. Scotland Yard was called in, Crippen and Le Neve fled to America, and their escape was foiled by modern technology. Their arrest was the result of the first use of the wireless in criminal detection. He was hanged. This story provides, roughly, the configurations for Collier's "Back for Christmas."

Like Crippen, Collier's hero is a doctor, although a rather more successful one than Crippen save in his own home. He, too, is married to a domineering wife, this one named Hermione, who manages his life and eventually, as he rationalizes it, manages herself to death. One of Collier's professionals, he has no moral difficulties with the taking of life into his own hands; like the dentist and doctor of "Another American Tragedy," he can find a rationalization for whatever act suits his needs.

As the story opens, Carpenter and his wife are saying farewell to friends. He is to go on a three-month lecture tour in America, and she is to accompany him. Mrs. Carpenter assures her friends that they will be back by Christmas, and the well-wishers are quite sure this will be true. In fact, the doctor himself, who has plans of his own, almost takes seriously her assurances since, for years, "she had been promising him for dinner parties, garden parties, committees, heaven knows what, and the promises had always been kept" (182). The well-wishers are also certain that Dr. Carpenter will thrive in America. His wife will take care of that.

The guests depart, and the doctor brains his wife, luring her into the bathroom so that the blood will go down the drain. Like Crippen, he then attempts to dismember her, but Crippen's wife had not the organizational ability of Hermione, who has turned off the water at the main. From this point on, the doctor is harassed by a hand from beyond the grave, until finally he manages to get his wife's remains into the cellar. Having buried her, he then leaves for New York. A woman waits for him in America, someone who is not aware that he is not already a widower. Carpenter adds a few Victorian touches in New York, typical of wife-murderers of a more leisurely age. He forges, for example, letters to her friends. But, like Crippen, he is foiled in the end. His *bête noire* is not technology but his late wife's efficiency. He is notified by a building contractor that his cellar is about to be excavated. Hermione has ordered a wine cellar for him, expressly requesting that it be finished in time for his return at Christmas.

"**De Mortuis.**" A physician also murders his wife in "De Mortuis," but this is a sad story, as well as an ironic one. In a few pages, it manages to reveal the hollowness of a marriage in which the partners may well not know each other at all and in which one, perhaps, does not feel free to be honest. There is both tragedy and comedy in the portrait of a doctor, presumably a scientist and thus a man of objectivity, who determines to murder his wife on the basis of evidence that would hardly be acceptable in the most inept of small-town police courts. And there is another kind of irony in the character of a small-town physician, traditionally a figure of human kindness, who values human life less than he values his reputation in the community and his standing in the eyes, especially, of the overgrown boys of the town.

At the beginning of the story, the doctor, described as being a "roughly constructed" man with the paws of an ape, is in his cellar patching the floor (9). His wife is absent. As he works, some fishing cronies arrive and, seeing the hole in the cellar, they assume that he has murdered his wife. They express sympathy with him and explain that they will never betray him. He has, after all, unknowingly married the loose woman of the town, a matter that they explain to him in the tones of the locker room or poker game. Perhaps telling the truth, perhaps partially telling the truth, perhaps showing off, they indicate that each has enjoyed the woman before her marriage to the doctor.

The doctor broods. After the fishermen leave, the door slams; it is his wife, returning. He lures her to the basement without allowing her a word in her own defense. She is last seen, a lonely figure, standing at the top of the cellar stairs.

"Wet Saturday."   This story is reminiscent of *Tom's A-Cold* in that the family pictured here is a small, paranoid clan waging war against the community outside its gates. Fearing for the loss of his standing in the community, the father of the family protects his insane and clearly dangerous daughter against the consequences of a murder she has committed and frames an innocent neighbor for the killing.

As "Wet Saturday" begins, the family is seen to be imprisoned by wet July weather; the rains are symbolic of the prison that the family has created for itself, for its members are trapped in a miserable and hateful set of relationships. The family is controlled by the father, who is deeply concerned with his status in the community. This can only be maintained by preserving his family intact, although he, Mr. Princey, privately despises his wife, his daughter, and his son.

In a rage born of envy and frustration, the daughter has just murdered the village curate. The curate has erred in confiding his dreams of marriage and a career to this dumpy, dowdy young woman who has mistaken his casual conversation for a passionate overture. When she discovers that he is proposing to a different woman, she murders him with, appropriately enough, a weapon from a family pastime, a piece from a croquet set.

The father calls the family together so that a way can be devised to conceal the murder. As they talk, Captain Smollett enters. Clearly, he is a longtime acquaintance, since he feels free to enter without knocking; it is also clear that he has overheard the conversation. Threatening the captain with a gun, the father forces him to leave fingerprints on the murder weapon and to fake evidence of his involvement in a fight. Grateful not to be murdered himself, the captain accepts Mr. Princey's word that the matter will go no further. Mr. Princey insists that his intention is merely to protect his family against any accusation by the captain himself, but, as Captain Smollett leaves, Mr. Princey is already on the telephone, reporting the captain to the police.

Thus, within the course of a single day, the family has condoned the murder of a man of god, broken a gentleman's agreement with a neighbor, and framed that neighbor, who, perhaps, will hang for a crime he did not commit. But the family and its reputation are intact. The sanctity of the home has been preserved. And an Englishman's home has once again proven to be his castle.

"**Midnight Blue.**"   This is another story of a family that conspires against the world at large. Here, the killer is an accountant, a fussy man so obsessed with structure and tidiness that, returning late to his home after murdering his business partner, he stops before a mirror to make sure his tiepin is straight before he begins to undress for bed. In his compulsive regard for ordering his world as he wants it, he also has become a bully. He is married to a plump, apparently good-natured and scatter-brained blonde of whom he is openly contemptuous. His children have sensed his attitude and they reflect it in their own attitudes toward their mother, who is alternately bullied and shouted down at the breakfast table.

The plot concerns the woman's dream. She has dreamed that her husband has murdered his business partner with his muffler and that, in the confusion, he has come home with the wrong muffler. As, amid interruptions, she manages to tell her story, a son runs in, saying that he has found a strange muffler in the hall.

The mother's character changes as the story ends. She calls the family together so that they can protect the father, but it is strongly suggested that the family's power structure has undergone a violent shifting. Until now, the family has been a prison for the wife and mother. The glint in her eye hints that it will remain one no longer. Now she will take her revenge for the years of his bullying.

"**The Chaser**" **and Other Tales of Adultery.**   Marriage vows often are broken in Collier stories, as is, perhaps, inevitable in the world he

envisions, in which loyalty and honor have been forgotten and acquisitiveness governs even relationships between people. To view another person as
property is, of course, imperfectly to see that person; it invites rebellious-
ness and unfaithfulness. Such an attitude also leads to murder in Collier's
world. Once people view their mates as objects to be owned and manipulated, then they feel free to rid themselves of these others much as they
might discard a fading suit or worn shoes.

Thus, in "A Dog's a Dog," the wife of an aging general arranges his
murder, hoping to acquire both her husband's estate and the young lawyer
who manages it. In "Bird of Prey," a family bird, the offspring of a parrot
and an eerie flying visitor, reveals to Emma Spalding's husband that she is
pregnant by another man and that she plans unscrupulously to pass off her
child as his own. He kills her. In "Rope Enough," a married couple,
neither of them particularly attractive, is bound together only by poverty
and by the husband's mastery of the Indian rope trick. With nasty
characters and such fragile bonding, it is inevitable that the husband is
tempted by an houri whom he meets at the top of the rope. And it is
equally inevitable that the wife should climb after him, spot a tempting
male figure reminiscent of Valentino, and ultimately arrange matters so
that parts of her husband's dismembered body fall back to the real world
below.

In "Three Bears Cottage," murder is the result of the search for
perfection. At the beginning of the story, despite the plot of the fairy tale
from which the title is taken, nobody is sleeping in anybody's bed. That,
in fact, would seem to be the problem. The husband and wife are living in
perfect isolation in a perfect cottage that lies isolated within a flawless
countryside. There seems to be no danger that anything will ever happen
to either of them. Once again, as in *Paradise Lost,* flawlessness and stasis
produce hell, and the couple is miserably bored. He dreams of a lady
younger than his wife; she is greedily eyeing a woodcutter down the road.
He attempts to poison her, but she, more cunning, arranges that he take
the poison himself.

"After the Ball" is a typically comic story about adultery. It concerns a
Mr. Dickinson and an inept devil who has come to earth to corrupt him.
Mr. Dickinson would seem to be uncorruptible, but what the demon
cannot manage is accomplished by a greedy wife, who sees Dickinson not
as a man but as a step toward social position. Before the wedding, she is a
wide-eyed and fragile secretary, but the demon is pleased, for he senses a
note of authority in her voice. After the wedding, she takes charge,

demanding more than her husband can provide and increasing her demands until he, once an honest cashier, is willing to accept money from any source. Her acquisitive instinct having run riot, it follows that she should want to acquire more than one man. Dickinson catches her with a lover and he kills.

Collier's stance is best seen in "The Chaser," a short and wistful story about a young man named Alan Austen. Austen is naive and he is very much in love. He wanders into a small, mysterious shop reminiscent of the shop in "Bottle Party," where the proprietor makes it known that he sells two potions. One, a love potion, is very cheap; it is that one that Austen wants to buy. The second is what the old man calls his "cleaning fluid" or "spot remover" (416). He simply wants to bring it to Austen's attention, he tells him; he knows Austen will not need it for many years. Austen cannot understand that he might ever need it. After all, he will give the love potion to his lady, and then he will have everything he wants. The old man is sure that he will. Austen's wife will love him obsessively. She will worry about him constantly, so much so that she seems to hover over him, and, if he strays, she will be hurt, but she will forgive him—eventually. She will lose her sense of humor and all her interest in life except for him, and she will never divorce him or give him grounds for divorce. To the young man, of course, this seems paradise, but the old man knows that such possessiveness and such permanence will become unendurable. The young man says good-bye as he leaves the shop. The old man responds with *"au revoir."*

Professional Men

Medical Men.   Murderous physicians, trained to believe themselves objective and contemptuous of human life, are, as has been seen, the villains of "De Mortuis," "Back for Christmas," and "Another American Tragedy," while a psychoanalyst, whose intellectual rigidity causes him to resemble a character from Moliére, appears in "Fallen Star." Another psychiatrist, cut from the same mold, figures in "Interpretation of a Dream," while a medical researcher ruthlessly manipulates a husband and wife in "Youth from Vienna." These figures all share certain traits—greed, the illusion of objectivity that conceals the reality of self-indulgence, overriding concern with self and status, and ridiculous faith that the rules they have been taught are sufficient to comprehend the universe.

Just as the psychoanalyst of "Fallen Star" alters all that he sees, including the mysteries of hell, to fit into his Freudian theories, so the psychiatrist of "Interpretation of a Dream" proves incapable of seeing the world
around him and of acknowledging that it includes the inexplicable. The
two men are alike, also, in that both mean well, which cannot be said of
Collier's medical practitioners.

The hero of "Interpretation of a Dream" is Charles Rotifer, a young man
employed in the office of an accountant in the same tall building that
houses a psychiatrist. Rotifer suffers from a recurring and horrifying
dream, and, being a man of imagination as the doctor is not, he senses that
it might foreshadow some unimaginable disaster. He dreams that he is
falling from his office window. As he falls past the psychiatrist's window,
he looks in, and he sees his fiancée sitting on the psychiatrist's lap. The
dream begins each time at a different stage of the fall.

Rotifer wants reassurance, and his appeal to the psychiatrist is a plea to a
witchdoctor who can exorcise the demons of which he is conscious. The
doctor is happy to oblige. Fussing with his ashtrays and refusing to discuss
anything but the dream itself, the psychiatrist invents explanations, the
fakery of which is obvious, and insists that his patient be comforted. It is
nothing but "a little neurotic compulsion—nothing that cannot be cured
in time," he insists (331). He recommends two or three visits a week. The
young man leaves.

The next patient is the fiancée. She too has dreamed, and her dream is
that she should visit this psychiatrist. When she sees him, she identifies
him as a father figure and jumps into his lap. There she is sitting when the
young man falls past the window.

The protagonist of "Youth from Vienna" is a scientist who wins a young
lady when she begins her acting career and loses her when she becomes
successful. He goes off to Vienna to study the function of the ductless
glands and returns, prepared to play god, in time for her marriage to a
glamorous tennis player. He gives them a wedding present, a single dose of
a drug guaranteed to provide eternal youth. Since both acting and tennis
playing depend on youth, he, casting aside his ethics, can then safely step
aside and wait to see the couple fight over the potion. Only after the
marriage is ruined does he admit that he has provided nothing but water.

Men of Law and Men of the Cloth.   Lawyers and clergymen are
less threatening in Collier's stories than are physicians, perhaps because
their positions in society limit them largely to sins of omission rather than
permitting them the more active vices. They may be fussy and compul-

sively concerned with order and ritual, but they do not mistake themselves for god. They are not killers.

Yet one of the most horrifying of Collier's stories is "The Tender Age," in which a clergyman proves himself utterly incapable of recognizing evil. The clergyman, Mr. Dodd, is speaking with a wanderer who has paused in the parish, a Mr. Renvil. The clergyman's small daughter is present. The stranger repeatedly observes that he loves small children; he describes them in the language of a *cordon bleu* cook. In response, Mr. Dodd talks about his work in the parish, which, in a fit of poesy, he describes as keeping away the Eternal Prowler. He sees himself as doing this by preaching sermons and by concerning himself with the work of the parish; he enjoys his garden and is totally uninterested in the imagination and the unknown. During the course of the conversation, he rejects as trivial such matters as novels and films, cannibals and cannibalism. Unquestioning of the stranger, whom he hopes will settle in the parish, Dodd encourages his daughter to walk out with the man into the woods. The stranger unencouragingly mutters that "no man can avoid his destiny."[1] Stranger and child leave together, and Dodd prepares to write his sermon.

The lawyer who is the principal figure in "Great Possibilities" does not unwittingly create disasters. He does, however, yearn to do so, if only he could assure himself that nothing important would be damaged. Like the murderer of "The Touch of Nutmeg .Makes It," the lawyer has lived so long with so rigid a system of rules and regulations that below his mild exterior a volcano simmers. He longs to be a firebug. Yet he can find nothing to set fire to. Finally he seems to have found the perfect eyesore, but, at the last minute, he discovers that if he destroys the house he will be destroying some of the most precious memories of his young manhood. He ends, to his own satisfaction, by buying the eyesore, establishing a rural fire department, and riding to blazes on the back of an engine.

The Commercial Mentality.   Most of Collier's greatest horrors take place in the realm of the businessman. Just as, in *Paradise Lost,* Satan sees the voices of future catastrophes born of technology, so does Satan's author look into the world of industry and hear the voices of countless victims. Industrialism and technology lead to brutality and pain, because they breed minds that see nothing but objects and, consequently, see people as objects to be manipulated.

"Evening Primrose" is probably Collier's most perfect story, flawless and unique. It is a narration by a poet, discovered sometime later by Miss Sadie Brodribb on a pad of paper purchased at Bracey's Giant Emporium.

A department store, of course, is the elysian field of the consumerist
society, and in this story a number of humans have quite literally made it
so.

The young poet has tried to escape from his tribulations by seeking
sanctuary in the store. To his surprise, he finds that he is not alone there.
The store is populated by a whole race of exiles who pose as mannequins
during the day and help themselves to whatever they want by night. Once
again, the poet is a misfit, for these are creatures who would sacrifice all
life, all art, and all normal human relationships for the sake of keeping
material objects around them.

As might be expected of their kind, they have established a status
system both within the store and among various stores with similar
inhabitants. That system is a microcosm of the system in the world
outside, being based on the expense and status of the store and of the goods
available. They are guarded by an eerie, terroristic police force whose
primary task, as in the world outside, is to repress rebels against a
property-oriented society. These weird figures function by turning living
bodies into actual mannequins; as in the world at large, human life is
unimportant as compared with the protection of property.

They are about to convert Ella into a mannequin. An innocent girl who
wandered into this population as a lost child, Ella has been held captive for
many years, serving essentially as a servant. She still retains her human
values, and she has made the serious mistake of falling in love with a night
watchman. This is enough to cause her to be condemned to death.
Ultimately, because the poet loves Ella, he attempts to defend her. Had he
succeeded, the note pad would never have been found.

"Witch's Money" is a similar story, although, because of the alien
setting and the innocence of the murderers, the story has a less chilling
immediate impact. In this story, money utterly corrupts a little town near
Perpignan when a painter moves in and rents a studio. He pays for this
with a check, an object which his landlord has never seen before. When the
peasant tries to cash the check, he finds he must pay a fee to the bank, and
he feels cheated. When the artist will not give him more money, he leads a
band of men from the town to the studio. There they kill the artist and
steal the remainder of the checks, which, in their innocence, they begin to
use among themselves as if the checks were cash.

Almost automatically, possession of these checks transforms the town
into a bourgeois society based on the values of the inhabitants of Bracey's
Giant Emporium. There are bargains and fancy clothes. Gambling is
immediately established, as is a bordello. Sordid marriages are made

between wealthy widowers and young girls and between young men and wealthy spinsters. The story ends as the men descend to Perpignan to cash the remainder of the unsigned checks. They are last seen entering the doors of the bank there, where they will undoubtedly find that the real world of finance is even more sordid and brutal than is their imitation of it.

The more power possessed by a man of commerce, the more apt he is to be a sadistic bully in Collier's stories. The worst of Collier's creations of this sort is the industrialist of "The Steel Cat."

The story itself concerns a feckless inventor on the edge of starvation who has created a new kind of mousetrap called a steel cat. He takes the worthless product to Chicago, hoping that he can market it although it is nothing more than a fake, completely dependent upon the cooperation of a carefully trained mouse. The mouse has become a pet. Even the black porter at the Chicago hotel where the inventor stays immediately becomes fond of the little animal.

Not so the industrialist. Spotting the invention for the fraud it is, the industrialist called in to look at the trap plays cat and mouse with its inventor. He will not permit the inventor to rescue the creature, who is drowning in a jar of water. The mouse dies, and only then does the industrialist maliciously ask to see the invention demonstrated again the next day. He leaves. The porter returns to share his precious food with the mouse. The poverty-stricken inventor, the porter in the run-down hotel, the dead mouse—these, it is implied, are the victims of the industrialist and his system, the real steel cat of the story.

In "The Invisible Dove Dancer of Strathpheen Island," a connection is made between this kind of mind and the mind of the common criminal. The villain of this story is an American businessman named Thomas P. Rymer, who may well have been named after a conservative eighteenth-century scholar and critic. The original Rymer wrote about *Othello,* which he regarded as trivial, saying that it should have been named the tragedy of the handkerchief and that it serves merely as a warning to wives to be careful of their linen. This later Rymer is also deeply involved with ladies' linen, being engaged in the manufacture of women's undergarments.

He is a crude and brutal creature, but he is caught up in the romance of Ireland, which he describes in the rhetoric of the Rotary Club, again evidencing Collier's sharp ear: " 'To me, as a business man,' said he, 'this is something like a bit of *Man of Aran* got into the *March of Time.* Boy! Look at those rocks! Look at that colour! Look at the birds!' " (359). Infected by the spirit of the countryside, however, he imagines that he sees a dove dancer among the many wild pigeons and doves. With the callousness of his kind, he immediately imagines the bust, waist and hip measurements of this mysterious creature.

What he wants, he must have. First he tries to bribe the dove dancer with diamonds, and, when nothing happens, he becomes enraged: "She's roused up the old cave man in me, that's how it is. I'm not claiming to be any sort of sheik, but this little Irish wonder lady's gotta learn she can't make a monkey of a straightforward American business man" (363). Finally, he disappears, and a dove lies dead. He has wrung the neck of the bird, just as he might have raped and murdered any woman who was so insolent as to reject his attentions.

Artists and Intellectuals.   There are two kinds of artists in Collier's world. Some pander to prevailing tastes. These are satirized in "Variation on a Theme," as well as in certain party scenes in *His Monkey Wife* and *Defy the Foul Fiend.*

They are also satirized in "Collaboration." Here, the principal figure is named Ambrose. He has an excellent life, divided between homes in New York and in the south of France, and he has an attractive blonde wife. When he loses his wealth, he determines to become an author merely to be able to maintain his standard of living.

Unfortunately, he is master of neither plot nor style. In New York, he finds an out-of-work writer whose technique approximates that of the gorilla in "Variation on a Theme." He can provide bloody and brutal plots, but he is no stylist. In France, however, Ambrose discovers a stylist. He deposits each of them in one of his homes and spends half a year in each place. He becomes a famous writer. His bored wife, taking her example from her husband, bears two children although the marriage previously has been childless. These infants are overheard in a rather compromising conversation in the yard. One is already inventing virile plots, while the other precociously transforms his brother's crudities into the elegance of a sophisticated style.

More often, artists are victims of the system, as is Eustace with his dummy in "Spring Fever," the poet who inhabits the store in "Evening Primrose," and the painter who is murdered by the townspeople in "Witch's Money." These artists conquer only when they abandon ordinary life altogether and make use of the magic that is their particular gift.

One successful artist is the hero of "Night! Youth! Paris! and the Moon!" Like the poet of "Evening Primrose," this man is exhausted with the world. To retreat, he sublets his studio and climbs naked into a trunk, where he lies when his tenant enters. What he thought was a man turns out to be an attractive woman named Stewart. Inevitably, she falls into the hands of a man who greatly resembles the brutal businessman of "The

Invisible Dove Dancer of Strathpheen Island." Invited to her studio on business, he makes overtures. His pride wounded when she rejects him, he assaults her and believes he has killed her. In a witty twist upon the "cute" meetings of lovers demanded of filmwriters, the villain then stuffs the girl's body into the trunk, where she lies naked on top of the naked artist. They meet. When the would-be murderer transports the trunk to Paris and opens it, the victims escape to a new life, killing him in the process.

Another victory occurs in "Possession of Angela Bradshaw," where the poet first appears as a disembodied spirit and plays havoc with a conservative middle-class home somewhat like that of Lucy Langton in *Defy the Foul Fiend*. The spirit first appears in Angela's bedroom, and, while this fails to worry Angela, it thoroughly distresses her narrow-minded parents and her stuffy fiancé. So rigid is this household, in fact, that Angela's mother, hearing of the ghost, assumes he must be a black ghost to be so lacking in a sense of the proprieties. Angela's fiancé withdraws with great haste from the engagement, since the freshness of the commodity can no longer be guaranteed. The breaking of that engagement delights both Angela and the spirit, who turns out to be a modern poet. He receives Angela's hand and a substantial marriage settlement. Angela's parents are too concerned with public opinion to do otherwise.

Victims of the System. Nowhere is Collier's touch more sympathetic than when he portrays people of no consequence, small people without pretensions who are caught between the gears of an industrial system and who are used as commodities by those who possess power over them. He evidences great sympathy with their plight and with their occasional explosions, and he is singularly compassionate in his handling of their adulteries and their murders.

The most moving of these stories is "Romance Lingers, Adventure Lives." It involves two married couples. Mr. Gosport and Mr. Watkins do not know each other, but they are neighbors in a suburb of identical houses in a world so devoid of meaning that even the shadows pose no threat. As the story begins, both men are coming home from work. The first of these figures, braced against the wind, seems less significant even than his shadow, while the second is described in terms that flatten the emotional landscape: "Around the bend, just out of sight, comes another figure, bowler-hatted also, scythe-curved also, also chopping its way through the icy air. It might be the shadow of the shadow. It might be Death. It is, however, only Mr. Gosport" (275).

As they walk along in isolated misery, Mr. Watkins considers robbing a bank, escaping to South America, and founding a harem. Mr. Gosport is more meditative. He contemplates all that he has read about the virtues of life in suburbia. He realizes that he and his ilk are the salt of the earth and the backbone of the nation and that "the Fairlawn Avenues of the world are its very jewels" (276). Nevertheless, he wishes that he were dead.

Each enters an identical home with a matched three-piece furniture set of a popular pattern. In each home, a wife is sleeping. In the morning, wives in familiar robes are cooking familiar breakfasts. The newspapers, however, are not identical, and it dawns on both men that they are in the wrong houses. But they have enjoyed their nights with a zest that both had almost forgotten. As they return to their homes, inventing excuses for their wives, they unwittingly pass each other. They find that their wives, who also have enjoyed their nights, are not prepared to check too closely on the reasons for their husbands' absences. Fairlawn Avenue now seems rather less monotonous.

Eventually, the families become friends and spend much time together. In suburbia, however, property is bound to raise its ugly head, and the couples finally are parted by a squabble resulting from the loan of a lawn mower.

"Special Delivery" is another such story, this one of a man who in many ways resembles the Edward Laxton of "Sleeping Beauty." The difference in the treatment of the hero here is quite significant. While Laxton is satirized in his search for perfection, Albert Baker is gently treated. He, too, wants the perfect woman. Not only does no such thing exist in life, but in Baker's case there is an additional problem. No flawless woman would be interested in a creature so insignificant as Albert Baker, who is no more than a window dresser in a store. In Laxton's case, the desire for perfection is pure egoism, tinctured with greed; in Baker's case, it is the poignant need of an invisible man to feel himself needed and to understand that he is loved. And so he falls in love with a department-store mannequin.

He has named her Eva after the mother of mankind. Her primary virtue is that she is utterly dependent upon him; she is the only person in the world who needs him. He dresses her each day and protects her, he thinks, against the leers of his coworkers in the store, and she cannot move a step without him. In return, he believes that she shares his dreams and understands him fully.

Naturally, he is ridiculed by his coworkers when they learn of his obsession, and he is forced to flee into the world outside. He takes Eva with him. By good fortune, he ends at the home of a wealthy artist, the only kind of man who can understand him and afford to befriend him with bemused compassion. Temporarily, he and Eva find shelter, but he bungles and is forced to flee with her again into the real world.

This time, he and his mannequin are not so fortunate. They encounter a group of thugs; once again, Collier creates the mentality of the businessman who strangles the dove or the would-be killer of "Night! Youth! Paris! and the Moon!" Mistaking Eva for a real woman with a perfect body, they decide to rape her; perfect things must be soiled. To do this, they must first get rid of Baker. They murder him, and, learning what Eva is, they toss the two bodies together into a quarry.

Collier's sympathy even extends to a murderer in "The Touch of Nutmeg Makes It." This killer, a statistician, is a compulsive obeyer of rules and signs; he does not have the status or the power to make the rules. Nervous and repressed, he is typical of Collier heroes, enmeshed in a world of law and formulae. He is a volcano, waiting to erupt.

Recently transferred to a mineralogical institute, he is befriended by two colleagues who remain sympathetic even when they learn he has recently been acquitted of the particularly bloody murder of a friend. He is touchingly grateful. When they meet socially, he wants to be honest with them, and he explains that he was acquitted only because the police could find no motive. He was asleep in the house, he claimed, when the crime was committed. He himself does not believe he killed his friend. He has no idea as to why he should have done so.

Gradually, his smoldering anger is revealed to his colleagues, who, at any rate, sense the disturbance of the rigorously disciplined and frustrated man. He begins to erupt one night as they discuss recipes for the evening's drinks. He feels—very, very strongly—that the drink he is mixing should be topped with nutmeg. As his friends watch helplessly, he suddenly starts to remember that other evening of drink-mixing and he looks with dawning horror at his hands. So does the reader, but the horror encompasses more than the killer. It is a horror for the rigorously structured life in a world that has imposed the full horrors of its wars and codes and rules upon a mere fragile human soul.

Chapter Eight
Radical, Craftsman, Visionary

Like E. M. Forster, John Collier did not believe in belief. He was sympathetic toward the human desire for an earthly paradise, for he was born into a world of Victorian values and studied the works of the Victorian visionaries, but he realized that the desire for a lost Eden is no more than a poignant dream. He was profoundly skeptical of the twentieth-century dogmas and ideologies that promise to make this dream come true, just as he was skeptical of a traditional theology that sought to restrict human behavior and cripple human aspiration for the sake of a paradise to come.

Collier's world view was that of a modern who accepts the Bergsonian concept of the world as process, flux, and change. To believe that some permanent order can be imposed on this universe is, at best, an act of self-deception. At worst, it is an excuse for authoritarian control of others and camouflage for those who want to manipulate others. Whether those who seek power for these reasons are Christian proselytizers or merely individual physicians or industrialists, Collier abhorred their ambition and attacked them. But, because he was a man possessed of a great love for life, a great hunger for experience, and a great capacity for enjoying all the riches of the earth, including the rich variety of human illusions and personalities, he attacked them with Rabelaisian laughter.

Even in the earliest of his writings, he expressed an understanding of the desire for a lost Eden. In *Gemini,* he allows Valentine to voice his own longing for the pastoral world of England lost in the fury of the First World War, and until the end of his lifetime he saw no better existence than that of a traditional English country gentleman in an age in which loyalties between master and man held strong and true. At the same time, he was a realist. If such a paradise ever actually existed, it was irrecoverable. In *Defy the Foul Fiend,* Corbo escapes back to what he thinks is such a life, but the pastoral dream crumbles under his hand. His paradise lacks an Eve, and his manor is not much better than a ruin. In *Tom's A-Cold,* Harry imagines such an Eden, but his dream is destroyed largely by the complexities of human personalities.

In later years, Collier returned to the theme repeatedly, increasingly showing the futility and even self-destructiveness of resting in that vision. Whether he was writing about the domestic perfection of "Three Bears Cottage" that leads to murder or the comic illusions of Edward Laxton in "Sleeping Beauty," he showed that, even were such a return to paradise possible, it would lead to a life that is no better than a vacuum, sterile and static. This, too, is a theme in his last work, *Paradise Lost,* in which God's paradise is seen as life within a bell jar under the supervision of a creator who, to preserve the status quo, must turn totalitarian dictator, intolerant even of that which he has created.

Connected with his concern for the lost Eden is his perception of the fragmented male personality. In *Gemini,* he expresses this concern through the dualities that he found in his own character; Orson, the man of action, and Valentine, the man of thought, appear again and again in his later work. He comes to see both traditional roles as illusory, just as the search for a lost paradise is merely an illusion.

The man of action, like Harry in *Tom's A-Cold,* will be thwarted by the complexities of human personalities and of the forces of change of which only the thinking man is aware, or he may look, like Adam at the end of *Paradise Lost,* for a simplified code of rules and regulations to impose upon others in order to make his own life bearable and his power complete. Or he even may become one of the tyrannical industrialists of "The Steel Cat" and "The Invisible Dove Dancer of Strathpheen Island," men who destroy that which is tender and beautiful because it defies their will. At worst, such a man is a villain; at best, he is the sad figure of Pierrot.

On the other hand, the man of thought too frequently thinks about the wrong thing. The protagonist of *His Monkey Wife* is a schoolmaster, yet he is profoundly ignorant of matters of sex and loyalty and love that lie at the core of human existence. Similarly, Crab, in *Tom's A-Cold,* has thoroughly studied the political theories available to him while remaining entirely unaware of the suppressed emotion inside him. Of the contemplatives, the creators possess the power of magic, but that rarely is enough, as is evidenced by the protagonist's plight in "Evening Primrose." Elsewhere, that power is exploited and abused; "Variation on a Theme" and Satan in *Paradise Lost* dissimilarly testify to that common point.

They lack the female; like Virginia Woolf, Collier came to realize the power of the female principle. It is the woman who understands the power of emotion and who looks through the political and religious constructs invented by man to see the realities of birth, sex, and death that lie below. In *His Monkey Wife,* Emily sees through the tinsel of civilization because she is a self-actualizing and autonomous being, not merely because she is an outsider, a monkey. Lucy in *Defy the Foul Fiend* is another such figure, as is Collier's Eve in *Paradise Lost,* and women like these appear sometimes even in the comic short stories, as when the powers of hell are helpless against Rosie's clear-eyed realism in "The Devil George and Rosie."

These elements—thought, action, nurture—do not come to full realization in any single character in Collier's writing. His world is a kaleidoscope or, perhaps, Shelley's dome of many-colored glass. As humans and events form patterns in the flux, occasionally the proper configuration appears for a moment, and it is possible to sense how humans might function effectively and joyously amid the flux. But mostly they do not do so, and, probably, nothing more than muddle is possible.

Collier's vision might well be one of despair and pessimism, but it is not, even though he is profoundly aware of man's mortality, of the desperation of thinking men and of the stultifying boredom and frustration of small men caught up in capitalistic machinery in which they are used as objects. What Collier stresses through his writing is the realization of the transience of all things, and he insists on stripping down the trappings of the world to bare essentials—time, sex, death, creativity. Granted awareness of these essentials, then a good life is possible, a life reminiscent both of a kind of existentialism and of those values that Collier inherited from his Victorian education and Edwardian boyhood—tolerance, loyalty, respect, dignity, affection, and, above all, pity.

But this good life is possible only to the man who is willing to remain an individualist, an outsider, roles that Collier accepted both in his life and in his writing. He belonged to no man and to no party, and he maintained his personal integrity and the integrity of his craftsmanship despite the temptations to which he occasionally and admittedly succumbed.

In the 1930s, having gained critical success in literary London with *His Monkey Wife,* he found himself repelled by the gray egalitarianism of political and common existence and by the commercialization of all life, including literary life. Abandoning his fashionable admirers, he fled to the country, making his position known both in "Please Excuse Me, Comrade" and in "Variation on a Theme."

During the McCarthy era, he found himself caught between two systems, and he was basically distrustful of all political systems. He could subscribe neither to the right nor to the left, despite his leftist sympathies and despite the cost to him in employment and in friendships. During the

1940s and 1950s, also, he found himself unable to pander to the commercialism of Hollywood, and he insisted, again despite the cost, on giving a higher quality of craftsmanship and scholarship than much of Hollywood was able to comprehend. And while doing this, he could not help but nibble playfully at the hand that fed him in such Hollywood stories as "Gavin O'Leary" and "Pictures in the Fire."

Throughout his career, he was willing to write for the popular media and to allow his stories to be made generally accessible through magazines of general appeal, but he would not compromise his personal standards in order to pander to the simplifications of popular taste. His craftsmanship, including his complex awareness of his literary tradition, is manifest in everything he wrote.

In the nineteenth century, his stance would have been termed that of a philosophical radical, and, indeed, he may have absorbed some of his attitudes from John Stuart Mill, who, he recalled, turned his mind toward socialism. Mill, of course, was raised in the utilitarian and laissez-faire tradition with which Collier's thought bears many similarities, and the feminist stance of both writers alike is similar. In "On Liberty," certainly, Mill expresses many of the concerns with freedom and its limitations that preoccupied Collier during much of his career. But in the twentieth century, Collier's thought would be regarded as what, in popular terms, is called libertarian.

Collier would be skeptical about calling it anything. Underneath all his writing lies, simply, the countryman's awareness of death as the central fact of life. As Paul Jarrico writes, Collier's purpose was "to confront our most profound fears, and to make light of them. Our fears of darkness, of the unknown. Our fear, in short, of death."[1] In the face of these dark facts, Collier seems to be saying, it is the quality of the individual life that alone is important. That life must be lived originally and creatively. If possible, it must be lived with nobility and integrity. Certainly, it must be lived with a weather eye always directed toward those who would limit it in order to aggrandize their own status and power. These attitudes, expressed with laughter, wit, grace, and style, are Collier's contribution to the literature of this time, and his is no small contribution. Although Collier was quite modest about his own literary achievements, Jarrico, and others, have observed that history will "rank him . . . among the best."[2] It seems probable that Collier's writing—witty, jaunty, honest, and clear-sighted—will be read and remembered when the literature that reflects merely the ideologies and the anxieties of our age is recalled only as an historical curiosity.

Notes and References

Preface

1. Anthony Burgess, Introduction to *The Best of John Collier* (New York, 1975), p. xii.

Chapter One

1. *Gemini* (London, 1931), p. 27.
2. Unless otherwise indicated in the notes, the quotations from John Collier throughout the text are transcribed from notes taken during two interview periods of several days each, one in July and the other in December 1979.
3. The great-grandfather was G. F. Collier. A number of his descendants were active in medicine, literature, and historical studies. Collier's sister, Kathleen Mary Collier, recalls that Vincent Collier, the uncle who acted as tutor to John Collier, was an "individualist like John." When young, he studied law and worked in a solicitor's office. He "acted for a Lady Helen someone in her divorce case; they fell in love and were to have married but she died. He immediately threw up his law work, retired to the home of his two unmarried brothers and two unmarried sisters and so far as I know never worked again." His one published novel is listed in the *British Museum Catalogue;* he worked for years on a massive novel that never was published; he never married and devoted much of his time to the education of John Collier.
4. Virginia Woolf, "Mr. Bennett and Mrs. Brown," *Collected Essays,* 4 vols. (New York: Harcourt, Brace, and World, 1967), 1:320.
5. Frederick Lewis Allen, *Only Yesterday* (New York: Harper and Brothers, 1931).
6. John Collier and Iain Lang, *Just the Other Day* (New York, 1932), p. 224. Lang was then a London newspaper editor, afterwards becoming editor of an English-language paper in India.
7. Martin Green, *Children of the Sun: A Narrative of "Decadence" in England After 1918* (New York: Basic Books, 1976).
8. *Gemini,* pp. 2–3. The apology and "Please Excuse Me, Comrade," cited below, are Collier's two primary autobiographical statements.
9. Allan Ross Macdougall, *The Gourmet's Almanac: Wherein is set down, month by month, recipes for strange and exotic dishes with divers considerations anent the*

111

cooking and the eating thereof, together with the feast days and the fast days and many proverbs from many lands also the words and music of such old-fashioned songs as should be sung by all proud and lusty fellows. To all this is appended a garland for gourmets tressed with many quaint fancies and literary blossoms culled from the most noble writers of all the ages (London: Desmond Harmsworth, 1931), p. viii.

10. Collier, ed., *The Scandal and Credulities of John Aubrey* (New York, Appleton, 1931), p. li.

11. The several quotations from filmwriter Paul Jarrico are from "Some Thoughts About John Collier," a talk delivered at a memorial service held on 13 April 1980 at the Collier home in Pacific Palisades. Mr. Jarrico is the author or coauthor of a number of films including *Tom, Dick and Harry, Thousands Cheer, The White Tower,* and *Assassination at Sarajevo,* and he produced *Salt of the Earth,* which won the Grand Prize of the Académie du Cinéma in Paris.

12. *New York Times Book Review,* 26 August 1979, p. 9.

13. *Books,* 5 April 1931, p. 6.

14. Stephen Spender, *The Thirties and After: Poetry, Politics, People, 1930–1970* (New York: Random House, Vintage Books, 1979), p. 13.

15. *New Republic* 67 (17 June 1931):134.

16. *Saturday Review of Literature* 150 (13 December 1930): 793.

17. *London Times Literary Supplement,* 5 February 1931, p. 96.

18. *New Statesman and Nation* 5 (8 April 1930):448; Jane Spence Southron, *New York Times,* 21 May 1933, p. 6.

19. Osbert Sitwell, "The Arts of Reading and Writing: Their Future," *Penny Foolish: A Book of Tirades and Panegyrics* (London: Macmillan, 1935), p. 326.

20. W. F., *Saturday Review* 155 (29 April 1933):413.

21. *Books,* 7 May 1933, p. 6.

22. *London Times Literary Supplement,* 27 April 1933, p. 292.

23. *Canadian Forum* 14 (September 1934):488.

24. *Spectator* 152 (8 June 1934):892.

25. *New Statesman and Nation* 7 (9 June 1934):886; *London Times Literary Supplement,* 14 June 1934, p. 422; *Saturday Review* 157 (23 June 1934):738.

26. F. B., *Chicago Daily Tribune,* 22 September 1934, p. 15.

27. Jarrico, "Some Thoughts About John Collier."

28. Other anthologies, which include *New Horizons in English* and *Understanding Fiction,* now make Collier's stories available to students of junior high school, high school, and college age.

29. Clifton Fadiman, Introduction to *The Touch of Nutmeg and More Unlikely Stories* (New York, 1943), pp. v–vi.

30. *New York Times Book Review,* 23 January 1944, p. 6.

31. *Nation* 152 (1 February 1941):136.

32. *Time* 37 (27 January 1941):76.

33. *The Best of John Collier,* p. xi. A selection from *The John Collier Reader,* this paperback edition, a similar edition of *His Monkey Wife,* and a Bantam edition of

short stories entitled *Fancies and Goodnights,* cited below, are the most accessible editions of Collier's work. Wherever possible, citations are to these editions.

34. Rupert Hart-Davis, *Hugh Walpole* (New York: Harcourt, Brace and World, 1952), p. 354.

35. Tom Milne, "The Elusive John Collier," *Sight and Sound* 45 (Spring 1976):105. Some of the material given to Milne was repeated, usually in the form of slightly different anecdotes and naturally in altered words, during the July and December 1979 interviews.

36. Ibid.

37. Michael Korda, *Charmed Lives: A Family Romance* (New York: Random House, 1979), p. 118.

38. Milne, "The Elusive John Collier," p. 106.

39. Ibid., p. 107.

40. Jarrico, "Some Thoughts About John Collier," p. 3.

41. Charlton Heston, *The Actor's Life, Journals, 1956–1976,* ed. Hollis Alpert (New York: Simon and Schuster, Pocket Books, 1979), p. 218.

Chapter Two

1. John Updike, "Milton Adapts Genesis; Collier Adapts Milton," *New Yorker* 49 (20 August 1973):84–85, 89.

2. Christopher Isherwood wrote this statement for the dust jacket of Collier's book; it was not used by the publisher. Collier carried the tribute with him until his death.

3. Virginia Woolf, *A Room of One's Own* (New York: Harcourt, Brace and World, Harbinger Book, 1957), p. 102.

4. *Milton's Paradise Lost: Screenplay for Cinema of the Mind* (New York, 1973), p. vii.

5. Bernard Shaw, *Back to Methuselah: A Metabiological Pentateuch* (Baltimore: Penguin, 1961), p. 25.

6. Cf. John Milton, *Paradise Lost,* I, 11. 254–55: "The mind is its own place, and in itself/Can make a Heav'n of Hell, a Hell of Heav'n." Frank A. Patterson, ed., *The Student's Milton,* rev. ed. (New York: Appleton-Century-Crofts, 1933).

7. Updike, "Milton Adapts Genesis," p. 89.

Chapter Three

1. John Fisher, *The Magic of Lewis Carroll* (Harmondsworth: Penguin, 1975), p. 11.

2. G. K. Chesterton, *The Man Who Was Thursday: A Nightmare* (New York: G. P. Putnam's Sons, Capricorn Books, 1960), p. 187.

3. Dudley Barker, *G. K. Chesterton* (New York: Stein and Day, 1975), p. 178.

4. S. N. Behrman, *Portrait of Max: An Intimate Memoir of Sir Max Beerbohm* (New York: Random House, 1960), pp. 228–29.

5. Nigel Nicolson and Joanne Trautmann, eds., *The Letters of Virginia Woolf, 1929–1931* (New York: Harcourt Brace Jovanovich, 1979), p. 14.

6. Alan Jenkins, *The Twenties* (New York: Universe Books, 1974), p. 214; Hesketh Pearson, *Bernard Shaw: His Life and Personality* (London: Reprint Society, 1948), p. 408.

7. Mary Girouard, "Lord Berners: Author, Artist, Musician and Wit," in *The British Eccentric,* ed. Harriet Bridgeman and Elizabeth Drury (New York: Clarkson N. Potter, 1976), p. 20.

8. *His Monkey Wife* (New York: Simon and Schuster, Pocket Books, 1975), p. 170.

9. Woolf, *A Room of One's Own,* p. 35.

10. Joseph Conrad, *Heart of Darkness and The Secret Sharer,* intro. Albert J. Guerard (New York: New American Library, Signet Classic Edition, 1950), p. 66.

11. Ibid., p. 67.

12. Ibid.

13. Ibid., p. 69.

14. Ibid., pp. 106, 114, 98.

Chapter Four

1. Elmer Davis, "Apocalyptic Literature," *Saturday Review* 10 (21 April 1934):642–43.

2. Samuel Hynes, *The Edwardian Turn of Mind* (Princeton: Princeton University Press, 1968), p. 34.

3. Ibid., p. 26.

4. Norman and Jeanne Mackenzie, *H. G. Wells* (New York: Simon and Schuster, 1973), p. 222.

5. "Please Excuse Me, Comrade," in *Ten Contemporaries: Notes toward Their Definitive Bibliography,* 2d ser., comp. John Gawsworth (London, 1933), pp. 109–10.

6. *Tom's A-Cold* (London, 1933), p. 113.

Chapter Five

1. *Defy the Foul Fiend or The Misadventures of a Heart* (Harmondsworth, 1948), p. 32.

Chapter Six

1. *Fancies and Goodnights* (New York, 1954), p. 215. Unless otherwise annotated, all future references to short stories are to this text, and the page references will be found within parentheses in the text.

2. H. H. Munro, *The Complete Works of Saki,* Introduction by Noel Coward (New York: Doubleday, 1976), p. 139.

3. *The Best of John Collier,* p. 413.

4. Bruno Bettelheim, *The Uses of Enchantment: The Meaning and Importance of Fairy Tales* (New York: Random House, Vintage Books, 1977), p. 8.

5. Andrew Lang, ed., *The Blue Fairy Book* (New York: Dover, 1965), pp. 54–63. This is a reprint of a work first published by Longmans, Green and Co. about 1889; it would, of course, have been one of the editions most readily accessible during Collier's childhood.

6. Louise Bernikow, *Among Women* (New York: Harmony Books, 1980), p. 8.

7. Ibid., p. 32.

8. Bettelheim, *Uses of Enchantment,* pp. 286–91.

Chapter Seven

1. *The Best of John Collier,* p. 467.

Chapter Eight

1. Jarrico, "Some Thoughts about John Collier," p. 5.

2. Ibid., p. 3.

Selected Bibliography

PRIMARY SOURCES

1. Collected Short Stories

The Best of John Collier. New York: Simon and Schuster, Pocket Books, 1975. Contains all stories found in *The John Collier Reader* but omits text of *His Monkey Wife*. Stories included are "Ah, the University!", "Another American Tragedy," "Are You Too Late or Was I Too Early?", "Back for Christmas," "Bird of Prey," "Bottle Party," "The Chaser," "Collaboration," "The Devil George and Rosie," "A Dog's a Dog," "Evening Primrose," "Fallen Star," "The Frog Prince," "Gavin O'Leary," "Green Thoughts," "Halfway to Hell," "Hell Hath No Fury," "If Youth Knew, If Age Could," "In the Cards," "Incident on a Lake," "Interpretation of a Dream," "The Lady on the Gray," "Mademoiselle Kiki," "Man Overboard," "Mary," "A Matter of Taste," "Night! Youth! Paris! and the Moon!", "Over Insurance," "Pictures in the Fire," "Possession of Angela Bradshaw," "Romance Lingers, Adventure Lives," "Rope Enough," "Season of Mists," "Sleeping Beauty," "Son of Kiki," "Special Delivery," "Spring Fever," "Squirrels Have Bright Eyes," "The Steel Cat," "The Tender Age," "Three Bears Cottage," "Thus I Refute Beelzy," "Variation on a Theme," "Wet Saturday," "Witch's Money," "Without Benefit of Galsworthy," "Youth from Vienna," and chapters 8 and 9 of *Defy the Foul Fiend*.

The Devil and All. London: Nonesuch Press, 1954. Contains six stories including "After the Ball," which does not appear in *Fancies and Goodnights* or in *The Best of John Collier.*

Fancies and Goodnights. Garden City: Doubleday, 1951. Reissued as Bantam paperback, 1954. Contains same collection as *The Best of John Collier* except for omission of "A Dog's a Dog," "Mademoiselle Kiki," "Man Overboard," "A Matter of Taste," "Son of Kiki," and "The Tender Age," and addition of "De Mortuis," "The Touch of Nutmeg Makes It," "Great Possibilities," "The Right Side," "Cancel All I Said," "Old Acquaintance," "Midnight Blue," "Little Memento," and "The Invisible Dove Dancer of Strathpheen Island."

Green Thoughts and Other Strange Tales. New York: Editions for the Armed Services, 1954. Reissue of stories previously published in *The Touch of Nutmeg.*

The John Collier Reader. New York: Knopf, 1972. Contents identical to *The Best of John Collier* except for inclusion of *His Monkey Wife.*

Of Demons and Darkness. London: Corgi, 1965. Abridged edition of *Fancies and Goodnights.*

Pictures in the Fire. London: Rupert Hart-Davis, 1958. Contains twenty-three stories, two of which do not appear in *The Best of John Collier* or *Fancies and Goodnights:* "And Who, with Eden . . ." and "Think No Evil."

Presenting Moonshine. New York: Viking, 1941. Contains twenty-four stories, all collected in *The Best of John Collier* or *Fancies and Goodnights.*

The Touch of Nutmeg and More Unlikely Stories. New York: Press of the Readers Club, 1943. Contains twenty-six stories, all reprinted in *The Best of John Collier* and *Fancies and Goodnights.*

2. Stories Individually Published

Green Thoughts. London: William Jackson, 1932.

No Traveller Returns. London: White Owl Press, 1931.

Variation on a Theme. London: Grayson and Grayson, 1935.

Witch's Money. New York: Viking, 1940.

3. Uncollected Stories

"Alien Corn." Manuscript, University of Texas Collection.

"Asking for It." *Playboy,* January 1975, p. 93.

"The Aviary." Manuscript, Harriet Collier collection.

"Col. Huneker." Manuscript, Harriet Collier collection.

"Conversation in Clare." Manuscript, Harriet Collier collection.

"Cupid Paid." Manuscript, University of Texas collection.

"Deferred Payment." *Collier's,* 27 April 1940, p. 12.

"Don't Call Me, I'll Call You." *Playboy,* September 1974, p. 143.

"Double Double." Manuscript, Harriet Collier collection.

"Egoisme a deux." Manuscript, Harriet Collier collection.

"The Elephant." *Esquire,* April 1935, p. 33.

"The End." Manuscript, Harriet Collier collection.

"Ever Bright and Fair." Manuscript, Harriet Collier collection.

"Faults on Both Sides." *New Yorker,* 21 July 1934, pp. 25–26.

"The Gables Mystery." *New Yorker,* 28 July 1934, pp. 15–16.

"Insincerity." *New Yorker,* 22 July 1933, pp. 13–15.

"In the Bag." Manuscript, Harriet Collier collection.

"The Last Infirmity." Manuscript, Harriet Collier collection.

"The Love Connoisseur." *Ellery Queen's 14th Mystery Annual.* New York: Random House, 1959.

"Love Divine Love." Manuscript, University of Toronto collection.

"The Mask and the Maiden." *Playboy,* January 1957, p. 47.

"Meeting of Relations." *Yale Review* 31 (1941):430–32.

"Mr. Thorwald's Kampf." Manuscript, Harriet Collier collection.

"Naked Truth in Viridian Springs, Arizona." Manuscript, Harriet Collier collection.

"Nice Surprise." Manuscript, Harriet Collier collection.

"None Are So Blind." *New Yorker,* 31 March 1956, pp. 29–34.

"Not Long Ago, Not Far Away." Manuscript, Harriet Collier collection.

"Patricia O'Brien." Manuscript, Harriet Collier collection.

"The Picture." Manuscript, Harriet Collier collection.

"Reindeer on the Way." Manuscript, University of Texas collection.

"The Roughest Shoot." Manuscript, University of Texas collection.

"Simply Appalling." *New Yorker,* 4 November 1933, pp. 15–16.

"Softly Walks the Beetle." *Playboy,* January 1960, p. 27.

"Sorine." Manuscript, Harriet Collier collection.

"Tangled Web." Manuscript, Harriet Collier collection.

"Things Seen." *Dial* 86 (1929):591–96.

"Till Death Do Us Part." Manuscript, Harriet Collier collection.

"Woodman, Saw That Tree." Manuscript, Harriet Collier collection.

"A Word to the Wise." *Esquire,* November 1940, p. 50.

4. Novels

Defy the Foul Fiend or The Misadventures of a Heart. London: Macmillan, 1934. Paperback reprint, Penguin, 1948.

Finding Ernie. Manuscript, University of Texas collection. Unfinished work. Collier had begun work again at time of his death; that copy in collection of Harriet Collier.

His Monkey Wife or, Married to a Chimp. London: Peter Davies, 1930.

Tom's A-Cold. London: Macmillan, 1933. Published by Appleton as *Full Circle.* New York, 1933.

5. Miscellaneous Works

An Epistle to a Friend. London: Ulysses Press, 1932.

Gemini. London: Ulysses Press, 1931.

Just the Other Day: An Informal History of Great Britain Since the War, With Iain Lang. London: Hamish Hamilton, 1932. New York and London: Harper, 1932.

"Lord Tennyson." In *Great Victorians,* edited by H. J. and H. Massingham. London: I. Nicholson and Watson, 1932.

Milton's Paradise Lost: Screenplay for Cinema of the Mind. New York: Knopf, 1973.

Preface to Allan Ross Macdougall, *The Gourmet's Almanac.* London: Desmond Harmsworth, 1931.

The Scandal and Credulities of John Aubrey. New York: Appleton, 1931.

Wet Saturday: A Play Adapted from the New Yorker Short Story. Boston: One Act [1941].

6. Unproduced Filmscripts
"The African Queen." University of Texas collection.
"Arabian Nights." Harriet Collier collection.
"Ballet Story." University of Texas and Harriet Collier collections.
"The Devil George and Rosie." Harriet Collier collection.
"Evening Primrose." University of Texas and Harriet Collier collections.
"Finding Ernie." University of Texas and Harriet Collier collections.
"Get Stuffed." Harriet Collier collection.
"Indian Summer." Harriet Collier collection.
"The Leatherstocking Saga." Harriet Collier collection. Adaptation of James Fenimore Cooper novels.
"Policeman." Harriet Collier collection.
"The Scavengers." Harriet Collier collection. Script written for Errol Flynn.
"The Secret Agent." Harriet Collier collection. Adaptation of Joseph Conrad novel.
"Sleeping Beauty." Harriet Collier collection.
"Time Stands Still." University of Texas collection.
"The War Lord." Harriet Collier collection.
"Wet Saturday." Harriet Collier collection.

SECONDARY SOURCES

1. Bibliography
Currey, L. W. *Science Fiction and Fantasy Authors: A Bibliography of First Printings of Their Fiction and Selected Nonfiction.* Boston: G. K. Hall, 1979, pp. 121–22. Lists collections of short stories, individually published stories, and novels.
Gawsworth, John. *Ten Contemporaries: Notes toward Their Definitive Bibliography.* Second series. London: Joiner and Steele, 1933, pp. 109–17. Contains Collier's essay "Please Excuse Me, Comrade," and technical bibliographic descriptions of first editions of *An Epistle to a Friend, Gemini, Green Thoughts, His Monkey Wife, Just the Other Day, No Traveller Returns,* and *The Scandal and Credulities of John Aubrey.*

2. Article
Milne, Tom. "The Elusive John Collier," *Sight and Sound* 45 (Spring 1976):104–8. Includes lengthy discussion of career as film writer and brief analysis of fiction writing.

Index